THE RESTAURANT BLUEPRINT

A GUIDE TO STARTING, SUSTAINING AND SCALING OF SUCCESSFUL RESTAURANTS

A BLEND OF DEEP PRACTICAL BUSINESS INSIGHTS AND STRATEGIC FRAMEWORKS FOR CULINARY ENTREPRENEURS AND PROFESSIONALS

A MUST-READ CULINARY BUSINESS COMPASS

DR. SURESH KAPITI
DR. TARAKESWARI POLAKI

Copyright © Dr. Suresh Kapiti, Dr. Tarakeswari Polaki 2024
All Rights Reserved.

ISBN
Paperback 979-8-89544-256-2
Hardcase 979-8-89588-259-7

This book has been published with all efforts taken to make the material error-free after the consent of the author. However, the author and the publisher do not assume and hereby disclaim any liability to any party for any loss, damage, or disruption caused by errors or omissions, whether such errors or omissions result from negligence, accident, or any other cause.

While every effort has been made to avoid any mistake or omission, this publication is being sold on the condition and understanding that neither the author nor the publishers or printers would be liable in any manner to any person by reason of any mistake or omission in this publication or for any action taken or omitted to be taken or advice rendered or accepted on the basis of this work. For any defect in printing or binding the publishers will be liable only to replace the defective copy by another copy of this work then available.

__To the Culinary Dreamers, Trailblazers, and Flavor Innovators:__

This book is dedicated to all the passionate souls who have made the world of gastronomy a vibrant and flavourful tapestry. To the chefs who turn simple ingredients into culinary masterpieces, the restaurateurs who create spaces where memories are made, and the dedicated staff who bring warmth and excellence to every table.

To my mentors and culinary inspirations, whose wisdom has seasoned my understanding and fuelled my ambition. Your guidance has been the secret ingredient in this entrepreneurial recipe.

To the loyal patrons who have dined at our tables, shared laughter, and created a community around the joy of good food. Your support has been the foundation on which this culinary venture stands tall.

To the late nights, early mornings, and the hustle that goes on behind kitchen doors – this dedication is a tribute to the hard work, determination, and love that every restaurant professional pours into their craft.

May this book serve as a source of inspiration, knowledge, and encouragement for all those who embark on the journey of owning and operating a restaurant. Here's to a world where every meal is a celebration and every restaurant tells a unique story.

With gratitude and a sprinkle of culinary magic

Dr. Suresh kapiti

&

Dr. Tarakeswari Polaki

Contents

About the Author

$\mathbf{M}$eet Dr. Suresh Kapiti is an earthling, hailing from the city of pearls Hyderabad (India). He is a committed entrepreneur, ESG expert, Author and a passionate advocate for professional growth and innovation.

Professional Journey:

With an impressive portfolio spanning across various domains, the author's career showcases a deep-rooted commitment to success. They have excelled in the corporate world, demonstrating expertise in Chemical, Mineral, Metal process Plant operations, Safety, Projects, Marketing & Sales. Their professional journey has led them to serve in different capacities, accumulating 13 years of valuable experience in major international firms. In addition to their corporate expertise, they have delved Business into diverse industries, dedicating 7 years to the fields of Restaurants (Hospitality), Exports, Mental Health, Manufacturing & Recycling Battery Metals.

A World Traveller:

An insatiable curiosity has fuelled our author's extensive travel experiences, spanning over 25 countries and gained insights, unique perspectives on global cultures and commerce.

Multi-Talented and Passionate:

In addition to their business acumen, the author is an avid reader, a teetotaller, a graduate of the Landmark Forum, a Toastmaster, and an advocate of epistemophilia (the love of knowledge). He is also a polyglot, reflecting their flair for languages, and serve as a Business Coach and Mentor.

Awards & Accolades:

Achieved the Distinguished Toastmaster (DTM) award from Toastmasters international (USA). The Distinguished Toastmaster (DTM) award represents the highest level of educational achievement in Toastmasters.

As a Director (Business leader role) of KAPITI OVERSEAS PRIVATE LIMITED (KOPL), Received award for implementation of Gender equality initiatives.

Financial Express recognized Visionaries of Pearl City (Hyderabad).

This book reflects not only the author's professional expertise but also his passion for Personal, Professional & Entrepreneurial development. Join them on a transformative journey as they share insights into 21st-century leadership in his profound and enlightening work.

✉ sureshkapitidtm@gmail.com

About the Co-Author

Dr. Tarakeswari Polaki, Founder & Director (Finance) at KAPITI OVERSEAS PRIVATE LIMITED (KOPL) & She is a seasoned Financial Professional.

Experience:

A serial woman entrepreneur, Tarakeswari is a Finance & Commerce professional with an impressive corporate background in Corporate Finance, Taxation, Business Valuation, Administration, and commercial activities. With 13 years of hands-on experience across diverse industries such as Manufacturing, Power Plants, Restaurant chains (Hospitality), and Exports, she brings a wealth of practical knowledge to the table and She serves as a Business Mentor.

Recognitions:

Recipient of honours from NFDB, IOD, Association of woman Entrepreneurs and FTCCI.

Financial Express recognized Visionaries of Pearl City (Hyderabad).

Dr. Tarakeswari is a Certified Corporate Director.

Passion for Exploration:

Beyond her corporate endeavours, Tarakeswari loves to wander and has explored over 10 countries.

This concise overview captures Dr. Tarakeswari Polaki's extensive experience, her dedication to the stock market for beginners, and her passion for financial education.

Contact: tarasuresh123@gmail.com

Foreword

Welcome to the world of culinary entrepreneurship, where passion meets precision, and innovation blends with tradition. In the pages that follow, you are about to embark on a journey into the heart of the restaurant business – an industry that thrives on creativity, dedication, and the artistry of food.

As someone deeply entrenched in the culinary landscape, I am honoured to introduce this comprehensive guide to the dynamic and ever-evolving world of restaurants. The Authors Dr. Suresh Kapiti and Dr. Tarakeswari Polaki are culinary entrepreneurs and seasoned experts in the area who provide not just priceless ideas but also a real passion for the culinary arts and the business that supports them.

Running a restaurant is more than just serving meals; it is a symphony of Flavors, a dance of logistics, and a delicate balance between customer satisfaction and operational efficiency. In these pages, you will find a wealth of knowledge covering everything from conceptualizing a unique dining experience to navigating the intricacies of marketing, staffing, and financial management.

What sets this book apart is its ability to seamlessly blend theoretical concepts with practical, real-world applications. The author's experiences, coupled with industry trends and case studies, provide a roadmap for both aspiring restaurateurs and seasoned veterans seeking to elevate their establishments to new heights.

Whether you are dreaming of opening your own eatery or looking to refine your existing operations, the wisdom within these pages will serve as a trusted companion. From menu planning to customer service, from managing the kitchen to creating a memorable ambiance, this book encapsulates the essence of what it takes to thrive in the competitive and rewarding landscape of the restaurant business.

So, prepare to immerse yourself in the gastronomic adventure that lies ahead. May this book ignite your passion, spark your creativity, and equip you with the knowledge needed to turn your culinary dreams into a thriving reality.

Bon appétit!

Dharam Singh

General Manager-Foodlink

India International Convention & Expo Centre (IICC-YASHOBHOOMI)

New Delhi, India.

Foreword

In the labyrinth of entrepreneurship, where dreams are nurtured, risks embraced, and passions ignited, there exists a distinctive and demanding realm — the world of culinary ventures. As we embark on the journey through the pages of "The Restaurant Blueprint: A Guide to Starting, Sustaining, and Scaling of Successful Restaurants," we find ourselves in the capable hands of two extraordinary individuals, Dr. Suresh Kapiti and Dr. Tarakeswari Polaki, who bring a wealth of experience and insight to the forefront.

Dr. Suresh and Dr. Tarakeswari have not only witnessed but actively shaped the ever-evolving landscape of the restaurant industry. Their journey is a testament to resilience, innovation, and an unwavering commitment to the pursuit of excellence. In this book, they generously share their combined expertise, offering a roadmap for aspiring restaurateurs and seasoned entrepreneurs alike.

"The Restaurant Blueprint " isn't merely a guide; it's a dialogue with mentors you wish you had when navigated the intricate tapestry of restaurant business. From the spark of an idea to the daily intricacies of managing operations, the authors seamlessly weave together practical advice, real-world anecdotes, and strategic insights.

As we delve into the chapters ahead, readers will discover a treasure trove of wisdom, distilled from the trials and triumphs of Suresh and Tarakeswari. Whether you're a culinary enthusiast dreaming of your own restaurant or an established player in the hospitality industry seeking to elevate your enterprise, this book is a compass that points towards success.

Beyond the nuts and bolts of managing a restaurant, the authors delve into the heart of the matter — the soul of a successful culinary venture. They explore the importance of fostering a unique identity, cultivating a loyal clientele, and staying ahead of industry trends. It's not just about running a business; it's about creating an experience, a destination that transcends the plate and resonates with patrons on a profound level.

Dr. Suresh Kapiti and Dr. Tarakeswari Polak invite you to join them on a journey that goes beyond the ordinary. Through their words, you'll find inspiration, practical guidance, and a deep appreciation for the artistry and business acumen required to turn a culinary vision into a flourishing reality.

So, let the pages of "The Restaurant Blueprint: A Guide to Starting, Sustaining, and Scaling Successful Restaurants" be your companion in this exhilarating voyage. May it empower you, challenge you, and ultimately pave the way for your own triumph in the vibrant world of restaurant entrepreneurship.

Bon appétit to your success

Anshuman

Entrepreneur, New Zealand

How to Read & Use This Book

The Intent of the book aims to provide valuable insights, guidance, and knowledge related to the restaurant industry. This book is helpful to approach it with a strategic mindset to extract the most valuable insights. Here's a guide to help you make the most of your reading:

1. **Preview the Book:**

    - Start by skimming through the table of contents and introduction to get a sense of the book's structure and main ideas.

    - Look for any summaries or key points at the beginning or end of each chapter.

2. **Set Objectives:**

    - Define your objectives for reading this book. What specific knowledge or skills do you hope to gain? Having clear goals will help you stay focused.

3. **Take Notes:**

    - Jot down key concepts, quotes, and ideas as you read. This can be done with a physical notebook or digitally.

    - Summarize each chapter in your own words to reinforce your understanding.

4. **Reflect and Relate:**

    - Consider how the concepts presented in the book relate to your own experiences or current challenges in your business or career.

    - Reflect on how you can apply the insights in your professional life.

5. **Engage Critically:**

- Evaluate the author's arguments and evidence. Are they well-supported and relevant? Don't hesitate to question and analyse the information.

- Consider alternative perspectives and viewpoints.

6. **Interact with the Material:**

- Engage actively with the content. Discuss the ideas with colleagues, friends, or online communities.

- Try to apply the concepts in real-world situations.

7. **Review and Summarize:**

- Periodically review your notes and summaries to reinforce your understanding.

- Create a brief summary of the entire book once you finish reading it.

8. **Implement the Insights:**

- Identify specific actions or changes you can implement based on the book's insights.

- Experiment with new strategies and observe the results.

9. **Read Critically, But Open-Minded:**

- Challenge assumptions and question the information presented, but also be open to new ideas and perspectives.

- Don't dismiss concepts outright; consider their potential value in different contexts.

10. **Recommend or Share:**

- If you find the book valuable, consider recommending it to colleagues or sharing key takeaways on professional platforms.

Remember, the goal is not just to finish the book but to absorb and apply the knowledge gained. Each reader may have a slightly different approach, so adapt these guidelines to fit your personal learning style and preferences.

Part 1

Business Introduction

Chapter 1

Introduction

The restaurant industry is a dynamic and diverse sector that encompasses a wide range of establishments involved in preparing and serving food and beverages to customers. It plays a significant role in the global economy and is a crucial part of the hospitality and service industry.

Food helps us feel wonderful. It is one of our most critical requirements. It serves both biological and social purposes. A meal is more than just eating; it is also about celebrating, bonding, spending quality time, relaxing, meeting new people, and providing entertainment and feeding the hungry.

With busier schedules and more discretionary cash, dining out at restaurants has become a common practice.

Food holds significant cultural, social, and emotional importance in human relations. It plays a central role in various aspects of human life, fostering connections, expressing emotions, and creating shared experiences. Here are some ways in which food is significant in human relations:

1. **Cultural and Social Bonds:**

   - Shared meals are a fundamental aspect of socializing in many cultures. Families and communities often come together around the dining table, reinforcing cultural bonds and traditions.

   - Different cuisines often represent cultural identity, and sharing or enjoying a meal from one's culture can be a way of expressing pride and connection to one's heritage.

2. **Celebrations and Rituals:**

   - Food is a key element in celebrations and rituals across different societies. Festivals, weddings, and religious ceremonies often involve specific dishes that hold symbolic significance.

- The act of sharing special meals during these occasions strengthens interpersonal relationships and creates lasting memories.

3. **Expression of Love and Care:**

   - Cooking for someone is often considered a gesture of love and care. Sharing a homemade meal can create a sense of intimacy and strengthen personal relationships.

   - The act of preparing and sharing food can be a way for individuals to express their feelings and emotions without the need for words.

4. **Business and Networking:**

   - Business meetings and negotiations are often conducted over meals. Sharing a meal in a professional setting can help break down barriers, build rapport, and foster a more relaxed and open atmosphere.

   - Networking events frequently include food, providing opportunities for individuals to connect on a personal level.

5. **Cross-Cultural Connections:**

   - Exploring and sharing different cuisines can be a bridge between people from diverse backgrounds. Trying new foods together can create a sense of adventure and curiosity, fostering cross-cultural understanding.

   - International cuisine and culinary experiences can bring people together, transcending language and cultural barriers.

6. **Comfort and Emotional Support:**

   - Comfort foods are often associated with emotional well-being. Sharing such foods during challenging times can provide solace and emotional support, creating a sense of solidarity.

   - Offering food to someone in distress is a universal way of showing empathy and care.

7. **Community Building:**

- Community events often revolve around food, from potluck dinners to barbecues. These gatherings strengthen the sense of community, promoting social cohesion and a sense of belonging.

- Food-related activities, such as community gardens or cooking classes, can bring people together with shared interests.

In summary, the significance of food in human relations is multifaceted, encompassing cultural identity, emotional expression, social bonding, and the facilitation of connections in various aspects of life.

Chapter 2

The Leadership of a Restaurateur

The leadership of a restaurateur is crucial for the success of a restaurant business. Effective leadership involves a combination of managerial skills, industry knowledge, and interpersonal abilities. Here are key aspects of leadership for a restaurateur:

1. **Vision and Strategy:**

   - **Vision:** A successful restaurateur should have a clear vision for the restaurant. This includes the type of cuisine, target audience, and overall atmosphere.

   - **Strategy:** Develop a comprehensive business strategy that includes marketing, menu planning, pricing, and customer service.

2. **Team Building:**

   - **Hiring and Training:** Selecting the right staff is essential. Hire individuals who align with the restaurant's culture and values. Provide thorough training to ensure employees are well-equipped for their roles.

   - **Motivation:** Inspire and motivate your team. Recognize and reward good performance to foster a positive work environment.

3. **Customer Focus:**

   - **Customer Service:** Prioritize exceptional customer service. Train staff to be attentive, friendly, and responsive to customer needs.

   - **Feedback:** Encourage customer feedback and use it to make improvements. Address customer concerns promptly and professionally.

4. **Financial Management:**

   - **Budgeting:** Develop and manage budgets for various aspects of the business, including food costs, labor expenses, and overheads.

   - **Profitability:** Monitor financial performance regularly and implement strategies to improve profitability.

5. **Adaptability:**

   - **Industry Trends:** Stay informed about industry trends, emerging technologies, and changing consumer preferences. Adapt your business model to remain competitive.

   - **Flexibility:** Be flexible and willing to make adjustments based on market demands and feedback.

6. **Communication:**

   - **Internal Communication:** Establish effective communication channels within the restaurant. Ensure that information flows seamlessly between management and staff.

   - **External Communication:** Develop a strong online presence through social media and other platforms. Communicate promotions, events, and updates to the public.

7. **Quality Control:**

   - **Consistent Quality:** Maintain consistent quality in food, service, and overall customer experience.

   - **Monitoring:** Regularly assess and monitor the quality of ingredients, cooking methods, and customer interactions.

8. **Regulatory Compliance:**

   - **Legal Compliance:** Stay informed about local health regulations, permits, and licensing requirements. Ensure the restaurant operates in compliance with all applicable laws.

9. **Innovation:**

   - **Menu Innovation:** Keep the menu fresh and exciting by introducing new dishes or updating existing ones.

- **Marketing Strategies:** Implement innovative marketing strategies to attract and retain customers.

10. Resilience:

- **Handling Challenges:** Restaurants face various challenges, from staff turnover to economic downturns. A resilient leader can navigate through difficulties, make tough decisions, and adapt to changing circumstances.

Successful restaurateurs often possess a combination of leadership skills, business acumen, and a passion for the culinary arts. Continuous learning, adaptability, and a commitment to excellence are key elements in the dynamic and competitive restaurant industry.

While the restaurant industry has quite a specific definition, it is worth remembering that there are still many different types of businesses that fall under the wider restaurant industry umbrella

Part 2

Types of Restaurants

Chapter 3

Fine Dining Restaurant

Afine dining restaurant is an upscale and luxurious dining establishment that offers an elevated culinary experience, distinguished by its high-quality food, exceptional service, and sophisticated ambiance. These restaurants typically have a more formal setting compared to casual or fast-food establishments, providing an atmosphere conducive to special occasions, celebrations, or intimate dining experiences.

Key features of fine dining restaurants include:

1. **High-Quality Cuisine:** Fine dining restaurants are known for their exceptional food quality, often prepared by skilled chefs who pay meticulous attention to detail. The menu may feature gourmet ingredients, creative presentations, and a focus on seasonal or locally-sourced produce.

2. **Elegant Ambiance:** The ambiance is an essential element of fine dining. The décor is often upscale and sophisticated, with attention to lighting, table settings, and overall aesthetics. This contributes to creating a refined and comfortable atmosphere.

3. **Formal Service:** Service in fine dining establishments is highly professional and attentive. Staff members are trained to provide a high level of service, including knowledge of the menu, wine pairings, and proper etiquette. Waitstaff may be well-versed in describing dishes, making recommendations, and ensuring a seamless dining experience.

4. **Exclusive Wine and Beverage Selection:** Fine dining restaurants typically have an extensive and carefully curated wine list, offering a diverse selection of wines to complement the menu. The staff may include sommeliers who assist patrons in choosing the perfect wine pairing.

5. **Reservation Requirements:** Due to the limited seating and high

demand, fine dining restaurants often require reservations. This adds to the exclusivity of the dining experience and allows the restaurant to manage its capacity effectively.

6. **Price Point:** Fine dining establishments are generally more expensive than casual or mid-range restaurants. The higher cost reflects the quality of ingredients, culinary expertise, and the overall experience provided.

7. **Innovative Culinary Techniques:** Fine dining chefs often employ innovative and cutting-edge culinary techniques to create unique and memorable dishes. Molecular gastronomy, precision cooking methods, and artistic presentations may be part of the culinary repertoire.

8. **Attention to Detail:** Fine dining establishments pay meticulous attention to every aspect of the dining experience, from the presentation of the dishes to the design of the menus. This attention to detail contributes to an overall sense of luxury.

Chapter 4
Casual Dining Restaurant

A casual dining restaurant is a type of eatery that offers a relaxed and informal atmosphere for patrons. These establishments typically fall between fast-food or quick-service restaurants and fine-dining establishments in terms of ambiance, pricing, and service. Here are some key characteristics of casual dining restaurants:

1. **Ambiance:** Casual dining restaurants usually have a comfortable and laid-back atmosphere. They may feature a mix of table and booth seating, and the decor is often inviting and casual.

2. **Service:** Service in casual dining restaurants is generally more attentive than fast-food establishments but less formal than fine-dining restaurants. Customers usually place their orders with a server, who may check in periodically throughout the meal.

3. **Menu Variety:** Casual dining restaurants often offer a diverse menu with a range of options, including appetizers, salads, main courses, and desserts. The cuisine may vary, including options like American, Italian, Mexican, or other popular styles.

4. **Price Range:** Prices at casual dining restaurants are typically mid-range. While not as expensive as fine-dining, they are generally higher than fast-food or quick-service options. This pricing structure reflects the quality of ingredients used and the overall dining experience.

5. **Alcohol Service:** Many casual dining establishments serve alcoholic beverages, including beer, wine, and sometimes cocktails. Some may even have a full bar.

6. **Open Seating:** Reservations are often not required, and customers can usually walk in and find a seat. However, during peak hours, there may be a waitlist.

7. **Family-Friendly:** Casual dining restaurants are often family-friendly, making them suitable for a wide range of customers, including couples, groups of friends, and families with children.

8. **Casual Dress Code:** Customers are generally not required to adhere to a strict dress code. While some may have a slightly upscale atmosphere, they are more forgiving in terms of attire compared to fine-dining establishments.

Chapter 5

Contemporary Casual Restaurant

Contemporary casual restaurants are similar to casual dining restaurants. Still, they emphasize aesthetics more to appeal to modern customers who may wish to take photographs of their meals and their dining experience for social media.

A contemporary casual restaurant typically combines modern design elements with a laid-back and comfortable atmosphere. Here are some key features and characteristics commonly found in contemporary casual restaurants:

1. **Modern Design**: Contemporary casual restaurants often feature sleek and modern interior design. Clean lines, minimalistic decor, and a neutral color palette are common elements.

2. **Open Layout**: The layout is usually open and spacious, creating a relaxed and inviting atmosphere. This design encourages a social and communal dining experience.

3. **Flexible Seating**: Versatile seating arrangements, including a mix of booth and table seating, allow for different group sizes and preferences. Comfortable and stylish furniture contributes to the overall ambiance.

4. **Casual Atmosphere**: The overall atmosphere is informal and relaxed. Guests should feel comfortable whether they're dressed casually or more formally.

5. **Open Kitchen Concept**: Many contemporary casual restaurants adopt an open kitchen layout, allowing diners to see the chefs at work. This adds an element of transparency and can enhance the dining experience.

6. **Innovative Menu**: The menu often features a mix of traditional and innovative dishes. There may be an emphasis on using fresh, locally sourced ingredients and experimenting with different flavor

combinations.

7. **Craft Cocktails and Beverages**: A well-curated drink menu is a common feature. This may include craft cocktails, local beers, and a selection of wines that complement the cuisine.

8. **Technology Integration**: Some contemporary casual restaurants incorporate technology, such as digital menus or ordering systems, to enhance the dining experience.

9. **Community Engagement**: To create a sense of community, these restaurants may host events, collaborate with local artists, or participate in community initiatives.

10. **Music and Ambiance**: Thoughtful selection of background music contributes to the overall ambiance. The goal is to create an enjoyable and lively atmosphere without being too loud.

11. **Casual Service**: The service style is friendly and approachable, emphasizing a casual yet attentive approach to customer care.

12. **Flexibility with Dietary Preferences**: Considering the increasing demand for dietary preferences and restrictions, contemporary casual restaurants often offer a variety of options to cater to different tastes and needs.

Remember that while these are common characteristics, there is always room for variation and uniqueness within the category of contemporary casual restaurants. The key is to create an inviting and enjoyable experience for guests.

Chapter 6
Quick Service Restaurant (QSR)

A quick-service restaurant (QSR) is a type of fast-food establishment that emphasizes speed and efficiency in service. Also known as a fast-food restaurant, QSRs are characterized by a focus on convenience, affordability, and a limited menu that can be prepared and served quickly.

Key features of quick-service restaurants include:

1. **Speed of Service:** The primary focus is on providing fast and efficient service to customers. This often involves streamlined ordering processes, quick food preparation, and rapid customer turnover.

2. **Limited Menu:** QSRs typically have a concise menu with a selection of popular and easily prepared items. This helps in reducing waiting times and simplifies kitchen operations.

3. **Affordability:** QSRs are known for offering relatively low-cost meals, making them accessible to a broad customer base.

4. **Drive-Thru and Takeout Options:** Many QSRs provide drive-thru services, allowing customers to place and receive their orders without leaving their vehicles. Takeout and delivery services are also common.

5. **Consistent Quality:** QSRs often focus on maintaining consistent quality and taste across their locations. This consistency is crucial for building brand loyalty.

6. **Limited or No Table Service:** Unlike traditional restaurants, QSRs usually do not offer full table service. Customers often place orders at a counter and may either take their food to go or find seating in a self-service area.

7. **Brand Recognition:** Many QSRs are part of large, well-known chains with strong brand recognition. This recognition helps attract customers and build trust in the quality of the food.

Common examples of quick-service restaurants include McDonald's, Burger King, Subway, Taco Bell, and KFC. However, the term can encompass a wide variety of establishments serving different types of cuisine, from burgers and sandwiches to pizza and fried chicken.

Chapter 7

Family Style Restaurant

A family-style restaurant is a type of dining establishment that typically offers a relaxed and casual atmosphere where patrons can enjoy a variety of dishes served in generous portions meant for sharing. This style of restaurant is often characterized by a warm and welcoming environment, making it suitable for families, groups of friends, and individuals looking for a comfortable dining experience.

Key features of family-style restaurants include:

1. **Shared Platters:** Instead of individual servings, family-style restaurants often serve dishes in large platters or bowls meant for sharing among the diners at the table. This encourages a communal dining experience.

2. **Comfortable Setting:** The decor and ambiance of family-style restaurants are usually designed to create a cozy and friendly atmosphere. This is to make patrons feel at ease and encourage a sense of togetherness.

3. **Varied Menu:** Family-style restaurants typically offer a diverse menu with a range of dishes to cater to different tastes and preferences. This may include appetizers, main courses, and desserts, ensuring there's something for everyone.

4. **Generous Portions:** Portion sizes in family-style restaurants are often larger compared to those in fine dining establishments. This allows guests to share and sample a variety of dishes during their meal.

5. **Kid-Friendly Options:** Many family-style restaurants provide kid-friendly menu items to accommodate families with children. These options are usually familiar and appealing to younger diners.

6. **Affordable Pricing:** Family-style restaurants often aim to provide good value for money, with reasonable pricing that makes dining out accessible for families and groups.

7. **Casual Service:** The service in family-style restaurants is generally informal and friendly. Staff members aim to create a laid-back and comfortable atmosphere for guests.

8. **Reservations or Walk-Ins:** Depending on the popularity and size of the restaurant, patrons may be able to make reservations or simply walk in. This flexibility makes it convenient for families and groups to plan their dining experience.

Examples of family-style restaurant cuisines may include Italian, American, Chinese, or Mediterranean, among others. Overall, the focus is on creating a welcoming environment where people can enjoy good food and each other's company.

Chapter 8

Fast Food Restaurant

Fast Food Restaurant

Fast food restaurants are focused on speed and convenience. While dining in is an option, most fast-food restaurants also provide a fast takeaway service, and many will provide drive-through service. The food is low-cost, and the ingredients' quality is likely lower than most other restaurant types.

Fast food restaurants are establishments that specialize in quickly prepared and served food. They are known for their efficiency, convenience, and affordability. Here are some key aspects about fast food restaurants:

1. **Quick Service:** Fast food restaurants are designed for speed and efficiency. Customers can typically place their orders at a counter, through a drive-thru, or via mobile apps, and receive their food quickly.

2. **Limited Menu:** Fast food menus often feature a limited selection of items, focusing on popular and easily prepared dishes. This helps streamline the ordering and cooking process.

3. **Standardization:** Fast food chains prioritize consistency in their products. This means that the same menu items should taste and look the same across different locations, ensuring a uniform experience for customers.

4. **Affordability:** Fast food is generally priced to be affordable for a broad customer base. This pricing strategy contributes to the widespread popularity of fast food, especially among budget-conscious consumers.

5. **Drive-Thru and Takeout:** Many fast-food restaurants offer drive-thru services, allowing customers to order and pick up their food without leaving their vehicles. Takeout options are also common, catering to customers who prefer to eat at home or on the go.

6. **Global Presence:** Fast food chains often expand globally, adapting their menus to suit local tastes and preferences. This globalization has led to the widespread recognition of popular fast-food brands worldwide.

7. **Health Concerns:** Fast food has faced criticism for its association with health issues, such as obesity and cardiovascular diseases, due to the often-high levels of salt, sugar, and saturated fats in some menu items. In response, many fast-food chains have introduced healthier options and provided nutritional information.

8. **Technology Integration:** Many fast-food chains have embraced technology, incorporating mobile apps, self-service kiosks, and online ordering systems to enhance the customer experience and streamline operations.

Chapter 9

Café

Cafes are small businesses in the catering industry that serve cheap and simple meals, including home-cooked meals, light snacks, baked goods, cakes and the like. While most restaurants emphasize food, most focus on serving beverages, including tea and coffee. The environment is free and the cafe can be converted into a cafe, house or tea house.

Cafés and restaurants are establishments that serve food and beverages to customers, but they differ in terms of their primary focus, ambiance, and menu offerings.

1. **Ambiance:** Cafés typically have a more relaxed and casual atmosphere. They are often known for their cozy and inviting interiors, with comfortable seating arrangements. Many cafés also provide outdoor seating options.

2. **Menu:** The menu at a café usually includes a variety of coffee and tea options, along with pastries, sandwiches, salads, and light snacks. Cafés may also serve desserts and baked goods.

3. **Service:** The service in cafés tends to be more informal, and customers may order at the counter. Some cafés also offer table service, especially for larger meals.

4. **Focus:** The primary focus of a café is on providing a comfortable space for people to socialize, work, or relax, often with a focus on coffee culture.

Chapter 10

Buffet Restaurant

A buffet restaurant is a restaurant that operates by placing food in a public area and allowing customers to help themselves and take the food to their tables. Brands in the restaurant industry tend to focus on specific dishes, but some offer a wide variety of options. Supermarkets often operate on an "all you can eat" basis, with customers paying for what they consume.

A buffet restaurant is a dining establishment where customers can serve themselves from a variety of dishes arranged on a table or a series of tables. Buffet-style dining is popular for its all-you-can-eat format and the wide range of food options available. Here are some key features and aspects of buffet restaurants:

1. **Self-Service:** Customers typically pay a fixed price and then help themselves to as much food as they desire from the buffet tables.

2. **Variety:** Buffet restaurants often offer a diverse selection of dishes, including appetizers, main courses, side dishes, salads, desserts, and sometimes beverages. This variety caters to different tastes and preferences.

3. **Casual Atmosphere:** Buffet restaurants often have a casual and relaxed atmosphere. Customers can choose their own seating and move around freely to select the dishes they want to try.

4. **Fixed Price:** In most cases, buffet dining involves a fixed price, allowing customers to enjoy a wide range of dishes without worrying about the cost of each individual item.

5. **Specialty Buffets:** Some restaurants may offer specialty buffets on specific days or during certain times, such as brunch buffets, seafood buffets, or international cuisine buffets.

6. **Popular for Large Groups:** Buffet-style dining is often popular for large groups or gatherings, as it allows people with different tastes to find something they enjoy.

7. **Cost-Effective:** Buffet restaurants can be cost-effective for both customers and the establishment. Customers get a variety of food for a fixed price, and the restaurant can manage food costs more efficiently.

8. **Common in Hotels and Cruise Ships:** Buffet dining is frequently found in hotels and cruise ships, offering guests convenient and flexible dining options.

9. **Hygiene Considerations:** Buffet restaurants must adhere to strict hygiene standards to ensure the safety and well-being of customers. Frequent replenishment of dishes, proper temperature control, and cleanliness are crucial aspects.

10. **Trends and Innovations:** Some buffet restaurants may incorporate trends and innovations, such as live cooking stations, themed nights, or interactive dining experiences, to enhance the overall customer experience.

It's important to note that the popularity and format of buffet restaurants may vary across cultures and regions. Additionally, the restaurant industry continually evolves, and new trends may emerge over time.

Chapter 11

Food Trucks and Food Stands

Food trucks and food stands are among the most informal options within the restaurant industry. These businesses operate a simple stand or food truck, where food is prepared and given to paying customers. The food options will usually be very limited and may even focus on one food item only, such as hot dogs, burgers, pizzas or local snacks.

Food trucks and food stands are popular elements of the food industry, offering a unique and often more casual dining experience compared to traditional restaurants. Here are some key aspects to consider:

1. Mobility:

- **Food Trucks:** These are mobile kitchens on wheels, allowing them to move to different locations. They often serve a variety of foods and can attend events, festivals, or set up in popular areas.

- **Food Stands:** These are stationary setups often found in busy urban areas, markets, or events. While not as mobile as food trucks, they are still flexible in terms of location.

2. Menu:

- **Food Trucks:** They can offer diverse menus, ranging from tacos and burgers to gourmet cuisine. The limited space means they often focus on a specific type of cuisine or a signature dish.

- **Food Stands:** Due to their size constraints, food stands may have a more focused menu, offering a specific type of cuisine or a few key items.

3. Cost and Investment:

- **Food Trucks:** Initial investment costs can be higher due to the need for a vehicle equipped with a kitchen. However, operational costs might be lower compared to traditional restaurants.

- **Food Stands:** Setting up a food stand may have lower initial costs compared to a food truck, but ongoing expenses depend on the location and the type of food served.

4. Regulations:

- **Food Trucks:** Regulations vary by location, and operators must adhere to health and safety standards. Permits are often required to operate in specific areas, and some cities have designated zones for food trucks.
- **Food Stands:** Similar regulations apply, and operators need to comply with health codes and other local regulations.

5. Popularity:

- **Food Trucks:** Became particularly popular for their novelty, diverse offerings, and presence at events. Social media often plays a significant role in promoting their locations.
- **Food Stands:** Commonly found in markets, busy streets, or popular tourist destinations. They may attract customers based on foot traffic and local reputation.

6. Customer Interaction:

- **Food Trucks:** Offer a more interactive experience, as customers can often see their food being prepared. Operators can engage directly with customers.
- **Food Stands:** Depending on the setup, there may be less direct interaction, especially if the food is pre-prepared.

7. Trends:

- **Food Trucks:** Have been part of culinary trends, offering unique and gourmet options. They often contribute to the "street food" culture.
- **Food Stands:** Embrace trends as well, adapting to the demands of local markets and preferences.

Both food trucks and food stands contribute to the diverse and dynamic landscape of the food industry, offering convenient and often affordable options for people on the go.

Chapter 12

Pop-Up Restaurant

A pop-up restaurant is a temporary dining establishment that "pops up" in a location for a short period, ranging from a single night to several weeks. These establishments are often found in unconventional or unexpected locations, such as warehouses, rooftops, art galleries, or even private homes. The concept has gained popularity as a way for chefs to experiment with new ideas, showcase their culinary skills, or test the market without the long-term commitment of a traditional restaurant.

Here are some key features and considerations for pop-up restaurants:

1. **Temporary Nature:** Pop-up restaurants are not permanent fixtures and are designed to be open for a limited time. This exclusivity can generate excitement and urgency among potential customers.

2. **Unique Locations:** Pop-ups often take place in unique or non-traditional venues, adding to the novelty and experience. This could include outdoor spaces, urban warehouses, or even industrial settings.

3. **Experimental Menus:** Chefs often use pop-ups to experiment with new and innovative culinary concepts, allowing them to gauge customer reactions and refine their offerings.

4. **Marketing and Promotion:** Due to their temporary nature, pop-ups rely heavily on effective marketing and promotion to attract customers. Social media, local press, and partnerships with influencers can be powerful tools in creating buzz.

5. **Collaborations:** Pop-ups frequently involve collaborations between chefs, mixologists, or other culinary professionals. These partnerships can bring diverse expertise and styles to the dining experience.

6. **Event Atmosphere:** Pop-ups often create a unique and event-like atmosphere, contributing to the overall experience.

This might include live music, themed decor, or interactive elements.

7. **Limited Reservations:** Due to the limited timeframe and often high demand, pop-ups may have a reservation system in place to manage the number of diners.

8. **Flexibility:** Pop-up restaurants offer flexibility for chefs and entrepreneurs to test their concepts before committing to a permanent location. It allows for agility in responding to market trends and customer preferences.

9. **Licensing and Permits:** Organizers must secure the necessary licenses and permits to operate a pop-up restaurant, ensuring compliance with local health and safety regulations.

10. **Customer Feedback:** Pop-ups provide a valuable opportunity for chefs to receive immediate feedback from customers, helping them refine their offerings and make adjustments.

Overall, pop-up restaurants offer a dynamic and exciting approach to dining, allowing both chefs and customers to engage in a unique and often memorable culinary experience.

Chapter 13

Cloud Kitchens

Cloud Kitchens

Cloud kitchens, also known as ghost kitchens, virtual kitchens, or dark kitchens, are a relatively recent and innovative concept in the food service industry. These kitchens operate without a physical storefront for walk-in customers and focus primarily on fulfilling online orders for food delivery or takeout. The concept has gained popularity with the rise of food delivery apps and the changing dynamics of the restaurant industry. Here are some key aspects of cloud kitchens:

1. **No Physical Dining Space:** Cloud kitchens don't have a traditional dine-in space. Instead, they are designed specifically for preparing food to be delivered or picked up.

2. **Online Presence:** Cloud kitchens heavily rely on online platforms and food delivery apps to connect with customers. Customers place orders through these platforms, and the kitchen fulfils the orders for delivery or pickup.

3. **Cost Efficiency:** Cloud kitchens can be more cost-effective compared to traditional restaurants because they eliminate the need for prime real estate locations with high foot traffic. This allows businesses to focus on the efficiency of their kitchen operations.

4. **Multiple Brands under One Roof:** Some cloud kitchens host multiple virtual restaurant brands operating out of the same kitchen. These brands might specialize in different cuisines or food types, allowing for a diverse menu without the need for separate physical spaces.

5. **Data-Driven Operations:** Cloud kitchens often leverage data analytics and technology to optimize their operations. This includes analyzing customer preferences, streamlining order fulfilment, and managing inventory efficiently.

6. **Flexibility:** Cloud kitchens offer flexibility to restaurant entrepreneurs and established chains. They can test new concepts or enter new markets without the significant upfront costs associated with opening a traditional restaurant.

7. **Rapid Expansion:** Because of their lower upfront costs and streamlined operations, cloud kitchens can quickly expand to new locations, responding to shifts in demand or targeting specific demographics.

8. **Challenges:** Despite their advantages, cloud kitchens face challenges such as intense competition in the online food delivery space, reliance on third-party delivery platforms, and the need to maintain high-quality food and service for off-premises consumption.

The growth of cloud kitchens has been accelerated by changes in consumer behaviour, advancements in technology, and the increasing popularity of food delivery services. This model offers a new way for entrepreneurs and established food brands to enter the market with reduced risks and costs compared to traditional brick-and-mortar establishments.

Part 3

Deep Insights of Restaurant Business

Chapter 14

Hygiene

Hygiene plays a crucial role in the restaurant business as it directly impacts customer satisfaction, food safety, and overall reputation. Maintaining high standards of cleanliness and hygiene is not only a legal requirement but also essential for the success and sustainability of a restaurant. Here are some key aspects of hygiene in the restaurant business:

1. **Food Safety:** Ensuring the safety of the food served is paramount. This involves proper storage, handling, and cooking of ingredients to prevent contamination and the spread of foodborne illnesses. Regular training for staff on food safety practices is essential.

2. **Cleanliness:** A clean and well-maintained restaurant creates a positive impression on customers. This includes cleanliness in the dining area, kitchen, restrooms, and all other areas accessible to customers. Regular cleaning schedules and procedures should be established and followed diligently.

3. **Personal Hygiene:** Staff members must adhere to strict personal hygiene standards. This includes practices such as regular handwashing, the use of gloves when handling food, and the proper wearing of clean uniforms. Employees with illnesses, particularly those related to foodborne diseases, should be excluded from handling food.

4. **Sanitation:** Regular sanitization of kitchen equipment, utensils, and surfaces is crucial to prevent the growth and spread of harmful bacteria. This involves using appropriate cleaning agents and following recommended procedures.

5. **Waste Management:** Proper disposal of waste, including food waste, packaging, and other materials, is essential for maintaining a clean and hygienic environment. Restaurants should have efficient waste management practices to prevent pest infestations and other sanitation issues.

6. **Pest Control:** Implementing measures to prevent and control pests is crucial for maintaining hygiene in a restaurant. Regular inspections, sealing entry points, and proper waste management can help prevent pest infestations.

7. **Compliance with Regulations:** Restaurants must comply with local health department regulations and standards. This includes obtaining necessary permits, undergoing regular inspections, and adhering to guidelines related to food safety and hygiene.

8. **Training and Education:** Ongoing training and education for staff on hygiene practices are essential. This ensures that all employees are aware of and follow proper procedures, reducing the risk of hygiene-related issues.

9. **Reputation Management:** A clean and hygienic environment contributes to a positive reputation. Word of mouth and online reviews can significantly impact a restaurant's success, and maintaining high hygiene standards is key to positive customer perceptions.

10. **Customer Confidence:** Customers are more likely to return to a restaurant where they feel confident about the cleanliness and safety of the food they are served. Hygiene practices contribute to building trust and loyalty among customers.

In summary, maintaining high hygiene standards in a restaurant is not just a legal obligation; it is a critical component of the overall business strategy. It contributes to customer satisfaction, protects public health, and helps build a positive reputation in the competitive restaurant industry.

Chapter 15
Freshness

Freshness plays a crucial role in the success of a restaurant business. It directly influences the quality, taste, and safety of the food, which are key factors in customer satisfaction and loyalty. Here are several aspects where freshness plays a significant role in the restaurant business:

1. **Quality of Ingredients:**

    - Fresh ingredients contribute to the overall quality of dishes. Using fresh produce, meats, and other ingredients enhances the flavor and nutritional value of the food.

    - High-quality ingredients can set a restaurant apart from competitors, attracting customers who appreciate the commitment to freshness.

2. **Taste and Flavor:**

    - Fresh ingredients often have more vibrant flavours compared to their processed or older counterparts. This can make the dishes more enjoyable for customers and lead to positive word-of-mouth reviews.

    - The use of fresh herbs, spices, and seasonal produce can elevate the taste of dishes, creating a memorable dining experience.

3. **Health and Nutrition:**

    - Fresh, unprocessed foods are generally healthier and more nutritious. Restaurants that prioritize freshness can appeal to health-conscious customers who are looking for nutritious options.

    - Providing fresh and healthy choices can contribute to a positive brand image, attracting customers seeking balanced and wholesome meals.

4. **Food Safety:**

- Freshness is closely tied to food safety. Maintaining strict hygiene standards and ensuring that ingredients are fresh and properly stored reduces the risk of foodborne illnesses.

- Adhering to food safety regulations is not only crucial for customer health but also for the reputation of the restaurant.

5. **Customer Satisfaction:**

- Customers often associate freshness with quality. A commitment to using fresh ingredients and preparing dishes to order can lead to higher customer satisfaction.

- Meeting or exceeding customer expectations for freshness can lead to repeat business and positive online reviews, contributing to the overall success of the restaurant.

6. **Seasonal Offerings:**

- Embracing seasonal ingredients allows restaurants to provide a variety of menu options throughout the year. This not only keeps the menu interesting for regular customers but also allows the restaurant to showcase the best produce available at any given time.

7. **Sustainability:**

- Fresh, locally sourced ingredients can be part of a sustainable business model. Supporting local farmers and suppliers not only reduces the environmental impact of transportation but also strengthens ties with the community.

8. **Menu Innovation:**

- Fresh ingredients inspire creativity in the kitchen. Chefs can experiment with new dishes and create innovative menu items based on the availability of fresh, seasonal ingredients.

In summary, freshness is a key factor in the success of a restaurant business, influencing the quality, taste, safety, and overall customer satisfaction. Restaurants that prioritize freshness can create a competitive edge and build a positive reputation in a highly competitive industry.

Chapter 16
Taste & Aroma

Taste and aroma play crucial roles in the success of a restaurant business, as they directly impact the overall dining experience and customer satisfaction. Here are some key aspects to consider:

1. **Customer Satisfaction:**

    - **Palate Pleasure:** The primary reason people go to restaurants is to enjoy good food. The taste of the dishes served is a critical factor in determining customer satisfaction.

    - **Memorable Experiences:** Exceptional taste and aroma create memorable dining experiences, leading to positive word-of-mouth and repeat business.

2. **Brand Identity:**

    - **Unique Flavor Profiles:** Establishing a distinct taste and aroma for your dishes can help your restaurant stand out from competitors. This uniqueness can become part of your brand identity.

    - **Consistency:** Customers expect consistency in taste. Establishing a consistent flavor profile helps build trust in your brand.

3. **Menu Development:**

    - **Balanced Flavors:** A well-balanced menu with a variety of flavours can cater to a broader audience. Consider offering options that appeal to different taste preferences, including sweet, salty, sour, bitter, and umami.

    - **Seasonal Variations:** Introduce seasonal ingredients to keep your menu fresh and exciting. This can also contribute to changing taste and aroma profiles throughout the year.

4. **Culinary Innovation:**

- **Experimentation:** Encourage your chefs to experiment with new ingredients, cooking techniques, and flavor combinations. Innovative dishes can attract adventurous diners and generate buzz for your restaurant.

- **Local Influences:** Incorporating local and regional Flavors into your menu can resonate well with the community and attract food enthusiasts.

5. **Ambiance Enhancement:**

- **Aroma in the Atmosphere:** The aroma in your restaurant is not solely dependent on the dishes but also on the overall atmosphere. Pleasant aromas can be created through the use of fresh flowers, herbs, or even specific scents.

- **Ambiance Matching Cuisine:** Ensure that the ambiance complements the type of cuisine you offer. For example, a cozy, dimly lit setting may enhance the experience for a romantic dinner, while a vibrant, energetic atmosphere may suit a casual dining concept.

6. **Marketing and Presentation:**

- **Visual Appeal:** Presentation is not just about how the food looks; it also involves how it smells. Appealing aromas can be highlighted in your marketing materials to entice potential customers.

- **Social Media Engagement:** Encourage customers to share their dining experiences, emphasizing the taste and aroma. User-generated content showcasing delicious-looking and smelling dishes can be a powerful marketing tool.

7. **Customer Feedback:**

- **Listening to Customers:** Actively seek and listen to customer feedback on taste and aroma. This information can help you identify strengths and areas for improvement.

- **Adapting to Trends:** Stay aware of food and flavor trends. Adapting your menu to align with these trends can keep your offerings current and appealing.

In summary, taste and aroma are integral components of the dining experience and contribute significantly to the success and longevity of a restaurant business. Consistently delivering exceptional flavours and aromas can lead to customer loyalty and positive reviews, ultimately driving the success of your establishment.

Chapter 17

Etiquette for Service

S taff etiquette is crucial in a restaurant business as it directly influences the overall dining experience for customers. Here are some key aspects of staff etiquette in a restaurant:

1. **Appearance:**

    - Uniforms should be clean, well-fitted, and in good condition.

    - Personal hygiene is essential. Staff should have clean hands, neat hair, and minimal use of strong perfumes.

2. **Greeting and Seating:**

    - Greet customers warmly and with a smile.

    - Escort them to their table and present the menu promptly.

    - Be attentive and observant to make the dining experience more personalized.

3. **Product Knowledge:**

    - Staff should be well-versed in the menu items, including ingredients and preparation methods.

    - They should be able to make recommendations based on customer preferences.

4. **Communication:**

    - Use polite language and maintain a positive tone.

    - Listen actively to customer inquiries and concerns.

    - Address customers by Mr., Mrs., or Miss unless given permission to use first names.

5. **Table Service:**

    - Serve from the customer's left and clear from the right.

- Be discreet and avoid interrupting conversations.

- Be attentive to refill drinks and clear empty plates promptly.

6. **Time Management:**

- Serve courses at a reasonable pace, ensuring customers do not feel rushed or neglected.

- Be aware of kitchen and bar timings to manage customer expectations.

7. **Handling Complaints:**

- Respond to complaints calmly and professionally.

- Apologize sincerely and offer solutions to rectify the situation.

- If necessary, involve a manager to resolve more complex issues.

8. **Teamwork:**

- Collaborate with colleagues to ensure smooth service.

- Communicate effectively with kitchen staff to avoid delays and errors.

9. **Payment Process:**

- Handle bills discreetly and efficiently.

- Thank customers for their patronage and invite them to return.

10. **Cultural Sensitivity:**

- Be aware of and respectful towards different cultural practices.

- Avoid making assumptions about dietary restrictions or preferences.

11. **Tidiness:**

- Keep the work area clean and organized.

- Regularly check and clean restrooms to maintain hygiene.

12. **Training:**

- Provide ongoing training for staff to enhance their skills and knowledge.

- Conduct regular briefings to update staff on new menu items or policies.

Remember that consistent staff etiquette contributes to a positive reputation for the restaurant, encourages repeat business, and can lead to positive reviews and recommendations.

Ambience

Ambience plays a crucial role in the success of a restaurant business as it significantly influences the overall dining experience for customers. A well-thought-out and appealing ambience can set the tone for the entire meal and contribute to customer satisfaction, loyalty, and positive reviews. Here are several ways in which ambience affects the restaurant business:

1. **First Impressions:**

   - The ambience is the first thing customers notice upon entering a restaurant. A welcoming and visually appealing atmosphere creates a positive first impression, enticing customers to stay and dine.

2. **Branding and Theme:**

   - Ambience is a key element in reinforcing a restaurant's brand and theme. Whether it's a casual family-friendly eatery or an upscale fine-dining establishment, the ambience should align with the restaurant's identity and target demographic.

3. **Comfort and Relaxation:**

   - Comfortable seating, appropriate lighting, and well-chosen decor contribute to a relaxing atmosphere. Customers are more likely to enjoy their dining experience when they feel comfortable in their surroundings.

4. **Cultural Influence:**

   - The ambience can reflect the cultural influences of the cuisine being served. This can enhance the authenticity of the dining experience and transport customers to a different place or time.

5. **Music Selection:**

- The choice of music can greatly impact the overall ambience. The right music complements the dining experience, while the wrong choice may create discomfort. The volume level is also important; it should allow for easy conversation without being too loud.

6. **Cleanliness and Maintenance:**

   - A well-maintained and clean ambience is essential for customer satisfaction. It contributes to the perception of professionalism and attention to detail, encouraging repeat business.

7. **Space Utilization:**

   - Efficient use of space is crucial. Crowded or cramped spaces can make customers feel uncomfortable, while well-spaced tables and thoughtful layout contribute to a pleasant dining environment.

8. **Social Media Appeal:**

   - A visually appealing ambience encourages customers to share their experiences on social media platforms. This can lead to positive word-of-mouth marketing and attract new customers.

9. **Dining Duration:**

   - Ambience can influence how long customers choose to stay. For example, a cozy atmosphere may encourage longer stays, while a fast-paced environment might be suitable for quick dining.

10. **Special Occasions and Events:**

    - A restaurant with a flexible ambience can cater to various occasions, such as romantic dinners, family gatherings, or business meetings. This adaptability enhances the restaurant's market appeal.

Investing in a carefully designed and well-maintained ambience can differentiate a restaurant from its competitors and contribute to long-term success by creating a memorable and enjoyable dining experience for customers.

Part 4

Start-Up

Chapter 18

Market Research

Market research for restaurants involves gathering and analysing information about the restaurant industry, target customers, competitors, and overall market trends. This research is crucial for making informed decisions about the business, such as identifying opportunities, understanding customer preferences, and developing effective marketing strategies. Here's a guide on conducting market research for restaurants:

1. **Define Your Objectives:** Clearly outline the goals of your market research. Are you looking to understand customer preferences, analyse competition, identify market trends, or assess the demand for a specific cuisine?

2. **Identify Your Target Audience:** Define the demographic and psychographic characteristics of your target customers. Consider factors such as age, income, lifestyle, preferences, and dining habits.

3. **Competitor Analysis:** Research existing restaurants in your area and those similar to your concept. Analyse their menus, pricing, marketing strategies, online presence, and customer reviews. Identify strengths and weaknesses in their operations.

4. **Location Analysis:** Evaluate potential locations for your restaurant. Consider foot traffic, nearby competition, accessibility, parking, and overall neighbourhood demographics. This information is crucial for choosing the right location for your target audience.

5. **Industry Trends:** Stay updated on current and emerging trends in the restaurant industry. This includes changes in consumer behaviour, popular cuisines, technology adoption, and health and sustainability trends.

6. **Regulatory Compliance:** Understand local regulations and licensing requirements for opening and operating a restaurant. This includes health and safety standards, food handling regulations,

and any permits needed.

7. **Customer Surveys and Feedback:** Conduct surveys or interviews to gather direct feedback from potential customers. Ask about their dining preferences, expectations, and what factors influence their choice of a restaurant.

8. **Online Presence:** Evaluate the online presence of potential competitors and assess customer reviews on platforms like Yelp, Google, and social media. This will give you insights into customer satisfaction and areas for improvement.

9. **Financial Viability:** Assess the financial feasibility of your restaurant business. Calculate startup costs, operating expenses, and potential revenue. Understand profit margins and break-even points.

10. **SWOT Analysis:** Conduct a SWOT analysis (Strengths, Weaknesses, Opportunities, Threats) for your restaurant business. This will help you identify internal and external factors that can affect your success.

11. **Networking:** Attend industry events, join local business associations, and network with other restaurateurs. This can provide valuable insights and potential collaborations.

12. **Consult Professionals:** Seek advice from professionals in the restaurant industry, such as chefs, marketing experts, and financial advisors. Their expertise can provide valuable guidance.

Remember that market research is an ongoing process. Regularly update your information to adapt to changing market conditions and customer preferences.

Chapter 19

Business Plan

Creating a business plan for a restaurant is a crucial step in establishing and running a successful venture. Here is a comprehensive outline for a restaurant business plan:

1. Executive Summary:

- Business name, location, and concept.
- Mission statement.
- Brief overview of the restaurant industry and target market.
- Financial summary, including funding requirements.

2. Business Description:

- Detailed description of the restaurant concept and theme.
- Type of service (casual, fine dining, fast-casual, etc.).
- Unique selling proposition (USP) and competitive advantages.

3. Market Analysis:

- Overview of the restaurant industry and trends.
- Target market demographics, psychographics, and behaviour.
- Analysis of competitors, including strengths and weaknesses.
- SWOT analysis (Strengths, Weaknesses, Opportunities, Threats).

4. Organization and Management:

- Legal structure (LLC, Corporation, etc.).
- Ownership structure and key personnel.
- Roles and responsibilities of each team member.
- Advisory board or mentors, if applicable.

5. Service/Product Line:

- Detailed menu description, including pricing.
- Sourcing of ingredients and suppliers.
- Any proprietary recipes or unique offerings.
- Future potential additions or changes to the menu.

6. Marketing and Sales Strategy:

- Target market analysis and segmentation.
- Branding and positioning strategies.
- Advertising and promotional plans.
- Online and offline marketing channels (social media, partnerships, etc.).

7. Funding Request:

- If seeking funding, specify the amount and purpose.
- Breakdown of how funds will be used.
- Repayment plan (if applicable).

8. Financial Projections:

- Projected income statements, balance sheets, and cash flow statements.
- Assumptions and methodology used in projections.
- Break-even analysis.
- Key financial indicators and ratios.

9. Appendix:

- Supporting documents, such as resumes of key team members.
- Any additional charts, graphs, or data relevant to the plan.
- Market research data and surveys.
- Legal documents (leases, licenses, permits).

10. Risk Analysis:

- Identification of potential risks and challenges.

- Strategies for mitigating risks.

- Contingency plans.

Remember to customize each section based on your specific restaurant concept, target market, and goals. Regularly review and update your business plan to adapt to changes in the market and your business environment.

Chapter 20

Legal Structure, Permits, Location and Lease

Establishing and operating a restaurant involves navigating various legal requirements, including choosing the right legal structure and obtaining the necessary permits. The specific regulations can vary depending on the country, state, and local jurisdiction, so it's crucial to consult with legal professionals or regulatory authorities in your specific location. However, here are some general aspects to consider:

Legal Structure:

1. Sole Proprietorship:

   - Simplest form, owned and operated by one person.

   - Full control but also full personal liability.

2. Partnership:

   - Owned by two or more individuals.

   - Shared responsibilities and liabilities among partners.

3. Limited Liability Company (LLC):

   - Provides personal liability protection.

   - Flexible management structure.

   - Pass-through taxation.

4. Corporation:

   - Separate legal entity with limited liability for owners.

   - More complex structure.

   - Subject to corporate taxation.

5. Franchise:

   - Operates under an established brand with support from a franchisor.

- Requires adherence to franchise agreements.

Permits and Licenses:

1. Business License:
   - Obtain a general business license from the local government.
2. Health Department Permits:
   - Ensure compliance with food safety regulations.
   - Regular inspections may be required.
3. Food Service Establishment Permit:
   - Specific permit for restaurants.
   - May include zoning and health-related requirements.
4. Alcohol License:
   - If serving alcohol, a separate license may be required.
   - Compliance with age restrictions is crucial.
5. Sign Permit:
   - Necessary for external signage.
   - Regulations on size, lighting, and placement may apply.
6. Building and Construction Permits:
   - Required for any structural changes or new construction.
   - Compliance with building codes is essential.
7. Occupancy Permit:
   - Ensures compliance with local occupancy regulations.
8. Music and Entertainment Licenses:
   - If hosting live music or entertainment, specific licenses may be needed.
9. Employer Identification Number (EIN):
   - Obtain an EIN from the IRS for tax purposes.

10. Employee Permits:

- Some jurisdictions require permits for employees serving food or handling alcohol.

11. Environmental Permits:

- Compliance with waste disposal and environmental regulations.

Always consult with legal and regulatory experts to ensure compliance with all local, state, and federal laws. Keep in mind that this is a general overview, and specific requirements can vary widely based on your location and the nature of your restaurant.

General overview of the common permits/licenses that restaurants in India typically need:

1. FSSAI License: The Food Safety and Standards Authority of India (FSSAI) issues licenses to ensure that the food served in restaurants complies with the standards set by the authority. There are different types of FSSAI licenses based on the scale and nature of the business.

2. Health/Trade License: Most municipal corporations or local health departments require restaurants to obtain a health or trade license. This ensures that the establishment meets health and safety standards.

3. Fire Safety Certificate: Restaurants, especially those with a certain seating capacity, may need to obtain a fire safety certificate to ensure compliance with fire safety regulations.

4. Signage License: Some local authorities may require a signage license for the display of restaurant signs, advertisements, or any outdoor displays.

5. Liquor License: If the restaurant intends to serve alcoholic beverages, it needs to obtain a liquor license. The process and requirements for obtaining a liquor license may vary across states.

6. Eating House License: In some states, an Eating House License may be required for any place where meals are served to the public.

7. Shop and Establishment Act Registration: This is a mandatory registration required under the Shop and Establishment Act,

which regulates working conditions and employment in shops, commercial establishments, and restaurants.

8. GST Registration: If the annual turnover of the restaurant exceeds the specified threshold, it is required to register for Goods and Services Tax (GST).

It's crucial to contact the local municipal or district office, food safety department, or relevant regulatory bodies in your specific location to get accurate and updated information regarding the permits and licenses required for opening and operating a restaurant. Additionally, it's advisable to consult with legal and business professionals to ensure compliance with all regulations.

Trademark & Logo

Registering a trademark and logo for your restaurant is a crucial step to protect your brand identity and distinguish your business from others. Here is a general guide on how to go about the process:

Trademark Registration:

1. **Conduct a Trademark Search:**

   - Before applying for a trademark, conduct a comprehensive search to ensure that the name and logo you want to register are not already in use or registered by someone else. You can perform this search through the official trademark databases.

2. **Identify Classes:**

   - Trademarks are registered in specific classes that represent different categories of goods and services. Identify the classes relevant to your restaurant business, such as class 43 for restaurant services.

3. **Prepare Application:**

   - Prepare the trademark application, including details like the mark, class of goods/services, and the owner's information. You can do this through the official website of the trademark office in your country.

4. **Submit Application:**

- Submit the application along with the required fees to the relevant trademark office. The application will undergo examination, and if no issues are found, it will be published for opposition.

5. **Publication and Opposition:**

- The trademark office will publish your application in the official gazette, giving others a chance to oppose the registration. If there are no objections, or if any objections are successfully resolved, your trademark will proceed to registration.

6. **Registration:**

- Once approved, you'll receive a certificate of registration. Trademark registration is usually valid for a certain period, after which it can be renewed.

Logo Registration:

1. **Create a Unique Logo:**

- Design a distinctive logo that represents your restaurant's brand identity. Ensure that it is original and doesn't infringe on existing trademarks.

2. **Combine with Trademark Application:**

- You can include your logo in the trademark application. Trademark protection generally extends to the specific representation of your mark, which can include words, stylized text, and graphic elements.

3. **Digital Format:**

- Submit your logo in a digital format as per the requirements of the trademark office.

4. **Use in Commerce:**

- To strengthen your trademark rights, use your logo in commerce. This means actively using it in connection with your restaurant services.

5. **Enforce Your Rights:**

- Regularly monitor the market to ensure that no one else is using a similar logo that could lead to confusion. If you find any infringement, take legal action to protect your rights.

Professional Assistance:

Consider seeking the assistance of a trademark attorney or agent to navigate the registration process. They can provide guidance, conduct searches, and ensure that your application meets all legal requirements.

Note that the process may vary by country, so it's important to follow the specific guidelines of the relevant trademark office in your jurisdiction.

Location and Lease

Finding locations and negotiating leases for restaurants, here are some key steps and considerations:

1. **Market Research:**

- Identify your target market and customer demographic.
- Research areas with high foot traffic and potential customer base.
- Analyse competitors and understand their locations.

2. **Zoning and Regulations:**

- Check local zoning laws to ensure the chosen location allows for a restaurant.
- Understand health and safety regulations, as well as licensing requirements.

3. **Budgeting:**

- Determine your budget for leasing a space.
- Factor in costs such as rent, utilities, and any required renovations.

4. **Real Estate Agents:**

- Consider hiring a commercial real estate agent with experience in restaurant leases.

- They can help you find suitable locations and negotiate lease terms.

5. **Lease Terms:**

   - Negotiate lease terms that are favourable for your business. Pay attention to factors such as rent increases, lease duration, and renewal options.

   - Understand common area maintenance (CAM) charges and who is responsible for them.

6. **Space Requirements:**

   - Ensure the space meets the requirements for a restaurant, including kitchen space, dining area, and restroom facilities.

   - Check for accessibility and compliance with disability regulations.

7. **Renovations and Customization:**

   - Factor in any necessary renovations or customization of the space to meet your restaurant's concept.

   - Negotiate with the landlord regarding who will be responsible for these costs.

8. **Due Diligence:**

   - Conduct thorough due diligence on the property. This may include inspections for safety, health, and building code compliance.

9. **Lease Negotiation:**

   - Work with a lawyer to review and negotiate the lease agreement.

   - Pay attention to clauses related to lease termination, renewal options, and any restrictions on the use of the space.

10. **Future Expansion:**

    - Consider the potential for future expansion and whether the lease allows for it.

Remember that the location of a restaurant can significantly impact its success, so take the time to carefully evaluate potential locations and negotiate favourable lease terms. Consulting with professionals, such as real estate agents and legal advisors, can be crucial in this process.

Chapter 21

Design and Layout

Designing and laying out a restaurant involves careful consideration of various elements to create a welcoming and functional space that aligns with the concept and goals of the establishment. Here are some key aspects to focus on:

1. Concept and Theme:

- **Theme Integration:** Ensure that the design reflects the restaurant's concept or theme. Whether it's a casual café, upscale dining, or a specific cuisine, the theme should be evident in the decor and layout.

2. Space Planning:

- **Traffic Flow:** Plan the layout to facilitate a smooth flow of traffic. Consider the entrance, waiting area, dining space, and restrooms to avoid congestion.

- **Zones:** Divide the space into functional zones (dining, bar, waiting area) with a clear purpose for each.

3. Seating Arrangement:

- **Comfort:** Choose comfortable and appropriately sized furniture. Consider the type of seating (booths, chairs, bar stools) based on the concept.

- **Flexibility:** Allow for flexibility in seating arrangements to accommodate different group sizes and events.

4. Lighting:

- **Ambiance:** Lighting plays a crucial role in setting the ambiance. Use a combination of ambient, task, and accent lighting to create the desired mood.

- **Natural Light:** If possible, incorporate natural light. It adds warmth and a connection to the outdoors.

5. Colour Scheme:

- **Branding:** Align the colour scheme with the restaurant's branding. Consider the psychological effects of colours on the dining experience.

6. Décor and Theming:

- **Art and Decor:** Incorporate art and decor elements that complement the theme. This could include wall art, sculptures, or unique features.

- **Branding Elements:** Use branded elements strategically but avoid overwhelming the space.

7. Kitchen Design:

- **Workflow:** Design an efficient kitchen layout to optimize the workflow for chefs and kitchen staff.

- **Ventilation:** Ensure proper ventilation to maintain air quality and a comfortable environment in the kitchen.

8. Technology Integration:

- **POS Systems:** Strategically place Point of Sale (POS) systems for efficient order processing.

- **Entertainment Systems:** If applicable, integrate audio-visual systems for entertainment.

9. Accessibility:

- **ADA Compliance:** Ensure the design complies with accessibility standards, providing ramps and proper restroom facilities.

10. Outdoor Spaces:

- **Terraces or Patios:** If applicable, design outdoor spaces that complement the overall theme and provide additional dining options.

11. Restrooms:

- **Cleanliness:** Maintain a high standard of cleanliness.
- **Design:** Extend the theme into the restroom design while ensuring privacy and comfort.

12. Sustainability:

- **Materials:** Consider sustainable and eco-friendly materials in the design and construction.

13. Regulatory Compliance:

- **Local Codes:** Ensure compliance with local building codes and health regulations.

14. Acoustics:

- **Noise Control:** Implement acoustic solutions to control noise levels, ensuring a pleasant dining environment.

15. Staff Areas:

- **Efficiency:** Design staff areas (server stations, kitchen entrances) to optimize efficiency.

16. Maintenance Considerations:

- **Durability:** Choose materials that are easy to clean and maintain.

17. Test and Iterate:

- **Pilot Phase:** If possible, conduct a pilot phase to identify and address any operational or design issues before a full-scale launch.

Always collaborate with experienced architects and designers, considering the unique needs of the restaurant and its target audience. Regularly review and update the design to keep it fresh and aligned with evolving trends and customer preferences.

Designing a restaurant kitchen is a crucial aspect of creating an efficient and functional workspace. A well-designed kitchen can enhance productivity, safety, and overall operational efficiency. Here are some key considerations for restaurant kitchen design:

1. **Workflow and Layout:**

   - **Zone Planning:** Divide the kitchen into different zones such as prep, cooking, cleaning, and storage. Ensure a logical flow between these areas to minimize backtracking and increase efficiency.

   - **Triangular Layout:** Arrange key work areas (cooking, preparation, and storage) in a triangular layout to reduce the distance between them, known as the kitchen work triangle.

2. **Space Allocation:**

   - **Adequate Space:** Allocate sufficient space for each workstation to prevent overcrowding and ensure smooth movement of staff.

   - **Separation of Duties:** Clearly define areas for cooking, food preparation, dishwashing, and storage to avoid confusion and enhance organization.

3. **Equipment Selection:**

   - **Efficient Appliances:** Choose commercial-grade, energy-efficient equipment that suits the restaurant's menu and volume of service.

   - **Ventilation Systems:** Install proper ventilation systems to maintain air quality, remove cooking odors, and ensure the safety of the kitchen staff.

4. **Storage:**

   - **Proper Shelving and Storage Units:** Install adequate shelving and storage units to organize ingredients, utensils, and kitchen equipment efficiently.

   - **Walk-in Coolers and Freezers:** Depending on the scale of the restaurant, consider installing walk-in coolers and freezers for bulk storage of perishable items.

5. **Safety and Compliance:**

   - **Fire Safety:** Adhere to fire safety regulations by installing fire suppression systems, proper extinguishers, and ensuring clear emergency exits.

- **Health Codes:** Design the kitchen in compliance with local health department regulations to maintain cleanliness and food safety standards.

6. **Materials and Surfaces:**

   - **Durable Materials:** Use durable and easy-to-clean materials for surfaces, countertops, and flooring to maintain a hygienic environment.

   - **Non-Slip Flooring:** Choose non-slip flooring to prevent accidents, especially in areas where there may be spills or water.

7. **Ergonomics:**

   - **Comfortable Workspaces:** Design workstations at comfortable heights to reduce strain on kitchen staff. Consider anti-fatigue mats to enhance comfort during long hours of standing.

   - **Proper Lighting:** Ensure adequate and well-distributed lighting to reduce eye strain and improve visibility.

8. **Technology Integration:**

   - **POS System Integration:** Integrate a Point of Sale (POS) system to streamline order processing and communication between the kitchen and front-of-house.

   - **Smart Kitchen Appliances:** Explore smart appliances and technology solutions to enhance efficiency and monitoring of kitchen operations.

9. **Flexibility and Future Expansion:**

   - **Modular Design:** Consider a modular design that allows for flexibility in case of future expansion or changes in the menu.

   - **Adaptability:** Plan the kitchen layout with the ability to adapt to evolving technological and operational needs.

10. **Consult with Professionals:**

    - **Kitchen Designers and Consultants:** Consider consulting with professional kitchen designers or consultants who specialize in restaurant kitchen layouts and can provide valuable insights based on industry best practices.

Remember that the specific needs of a restaurant kitchen can vary based on the type of cuisine, volume of service, and available space. Customizing the design to meet the unique requirements of the restaurant is essential for creating a successful and efficient kitchen.

Chapter 22
Menu Development

Menu development is a crucial aspect of creating a successful restaurant. A well-crafted menu not only showcases the culinary identity of the establishment but also plays a significant role in attracting and retaining customers. Here's a step-by-step guide to help you with menu development:

1. Define Your Concept:

- Clearly define your restaurant concept. Is it fine dining, casual, ethnic, fast-casual, or something else?

- Understand your target audience and their preferences.

2. Research the Market:

- Analyze competitors' menus to identify popular and unique dishes.

- Consider pricing strategies and portion sizes.

3. Create a Theme:

- Develop a cohesive theme for your menu. It could be based on cuisine, region, or a unique concept.

4. Determine Menu Categories:

- Structure your menu with logical categories (appetizers, mains, desserts, etc.).

- Consider dietary preferences, such as vegetarian, vegan, or gluten-free options.

5. Balance and Variety:

- Ensure a balance of flavors, textures, and colors.

- Provide a variety of options to cater to different tastes.

6. Signature Dishes:

- Highlight a few signature dishes that represent the essence of your restaurant.

- Make sure these dishes are unique and memorable.

7. Seasonal and Local Ingredients:

- Incorporate seasonal and locally-sourced ingredients for freshness and sustainability.
- Highlight these aspects on the menu for marketing.

8. Menu Layout and Design:

- Create an easily readable and aesthetically pleasing menu layout.
- Use high-quality images and descriptive language for each dish.

9. Pricing Strategy:

- Set competitive prices based on food costs, labor, and overhead.
- Consider psychological pricing strategies (e.g., $9.99 instead of $10).

10. Specials and Limited-Time Offers:

- Introduce specials or limited-time offers to create excitement and encourage repeat visits.

11. Beverage Program:

- Develop a well-curated beverage menu (alcoholic and non-alcoholic).
- Consider unique cocktails, a diverse wine list, and craft beverages.

12. Training Staff:

- Ensure staff is well-trained on the menu, including ingredients and preparation methods.
- Encourage them to make recommendations based on customer preferences.

13. Feedback Mechanism:

- Establish a system for collecting customer feedback on the menu.
- Use feedback to make necessary adjustments and improvements.

14. Menu Updates:

- Regularly review and update the menu to keep it fresh and exciting.

- Introduce seasonal changes or new dishes to maintain customer interest.

15. Legal Considerations:

- Ensure compliance with health and safety regulations.
- Clearly list allergens and provide accurate nutritional information if required.

Remember, flexibility is key. Continuously monitor the performance of dishes, gather feedback, and be willing to make adjustments to meet customer expectations and industry trends.

Chapter 23

Suppliers and Inventory

To obtain the inventory of a restaurant from suppliers, you typically follow these steps:

1. **Contact Suppliers:** Reach out to the various suppliers with whom the restaurant has established relationships. These suppliers could include those providing food items, beverages, kitchen equipment, utensils, cleaning supplies, and more.

2. **Request Inventory Lists:** Ask each supplier to provide you with an updated inventory list. This list should detail the products they supply, along with quantities and possibly expiration dates.

3. **Use Electronic Systems:** Many modern restaurants and suppliers use electronic systems for inventory management. In such cases, you may be able to access the inventory lists through online portals, software, or other electronic means.

4. **Regular Communication:** Establish a regular communication schedule with suppliers to ensure you are informed about any changes in inventory, such as new products, discontinued items, or changes in pricing.

5. **Review Invoices and Delivery Records:** In addition to directly asking for inventory lists, review invoices and delivery records from suppliers. These documents can also provide information on the items received and their quantities.

6. **Implement Technology Solutions:** Some restaurants use technology solutions such as inventory management software to streamline the process. These tools can help automate the tracking of inventory levels and provide real-time information.

7. **Physical Counts:** Conduct periodic physical counts of the inventory within the restaurant. Compare these counts with the information provided by suppliers to identify any discrepancies.

8. **Forecasting and Planning:** Use the inventory information to forecast demand and plan orders accordingly. This helps in maintaining optimal stock levels and avoiding shortages.

9. **Negotiate Terms and Prices:** Regularly review and negotiate terms and prices with suppliers to ensure that the restaurant is getting the best deals and maintaining cost-efficiency.

10. **Monitor Trends and Market Conditions:** Stay informed about industry trends and market conditions that might affect the availability and pricing of certain items. This information can help in making proactive decisions about inventory management.

By following these steps and maintaining good communication with suppliers, a restaurant can effectively manage its inventory and ensure a smooth and efficient operation.

Chapter 24
Equipment and Technology

The equipment and technology used in restaurants can vary based on the type of cuisine, size of the establishment, and the level of automation desired. Here are some common elements found in restaurant operations:

1. **Kitchen Equipment:**

   - **Cooking Appliances:** Stoves, ovens, grills, fryers, microwaves, and sous-vide machines.

   - **Refrigeration:** Walk-in coolers, freezers, refrigerators, and blast chillers.

   - **Food Preparation:** Cutting boards, knives, food processors, mixers, blenders, and slicers.

   - **Dishwashing:** Dishwashers, sinks, and drying racks.

2. **Point of Sale (POS) Systems:**

   - **Ordering System:** Touchscreen terminals or tablets for order entry.

   - **Payment Processing:** Integrated card readers or contactless payment options.

   - **Inventory Management:** Tracks stock levels and automates reordering.

   - **Customer Relationship Management (CRM):** Manages customer data and preferences.

3. **Reservation Systems:**

   - **Online Booking Platforms:** Websites or mobile apps for customers to make reservations.

   - **Reservation Management:** Tools for tracking and managing reservations.

4. **Communication Systems:**

- **Intercom Systems:** Connects kitchen and front-of-house staff.

- **Messaging Apps:** Internal communication tools for staff coordination.

5. **Security Systems:**

- **Surveillance Cameras:** Monitor dining areas, kitchens, and entry points.

- **Access Control:** Secure areas with restricted access.

6. **Digital Menu Boards:**

- **Electronic Displays:** Dynamic menu boards that can be updated easily.

- **QR Code Menus:** Allows customers to view menus on their smartphones.

7. **Inventory Management Systems:**

- **Tracking Software:** Monitors stock levels, reduces waste, and automates reordering.

- **Barcode Scanners:** Speeds up the process of checking in new inventory.

8. **Staff Scheduling Software:**

- **Employee Scheduling Tools:** Streamlines scheduling and tracks working hours.

9. **Online Ordering and Delivery Platforms:**

- **Third-Party Apps:** Platforms like Uber Eats, DoorDash, or Grubhub for online orders.

- **In-House Delivery Systems:** Restaurant-specific delivery services.

10. **Wireless Technology:**

- **Wi-Fi:** Provides internet access for customers and staff.

- **Mobile Devices:** Tablets or smartphones for order processing and communication.

11. **Automation Systems:**

- **Kitchen Automation:** Systems that streamline cooking processes.

- **Robotic Kitchen Appliances:** Automated machines for specific cooking tasks.

12. **Temperature Control Systems:**

- **HVAC Systems:** Heating, ventilation, and air conditioning for comfort.

- **Temperature Monitoring:** Ensures food safety in storage areas.

13. **Training and Employee Management:**

- **Learning Management Systems (LMS):** Online platforms for employee training.

- **Human Resources Software:** Manages employee data, payroll, and benefits.

The specific technology and equipment a restaurant uses depend on its scale, budget, and the desired level of automation and efficiency. Modern restaurants often integrate various technologies to enhance customer experience, streamline operations, and stay competitive in the industry.

Chapter 25

Hiring and Training

Hiring and training restaurant staff are critical aspects of running a successful restaurant. Here's a guide to help you through the process:

Hiring:

1. **Define Job Roles:**

   - Clearly outline the roles and responsibilities for each position (servers, cooks, hosts, etc.).

   - Determine the number of staff required for each role based on the size and type of your restaurant.

2. **Create Job Descriptions:**

   - Develop detailed job descriptions outlining the skills, qualifications, and responsibilities for each position.

   - Highlight any specific requirements such as experience in the food industry or customer service skills.

3. **Advertise Job Openings:**

   - Utilize various platforms such as job boards, social media, and your restaurant's website to advertise job openings.

   - Consider local community boards and culinary schools for potential candidates.

4. **Review Resumes and Applications:**

   - Screen resumes and applications to shortlist candidates who meet the necessary criteria.

   - Look for relevant experience, skills, and a positive attitude.

5. **Conduct Interviews:**

   - Conduct thorough interviews to assess candidates' interpersonal skills, problem-solving abilities, and their fit within the team.

- Consider holding practical or role-specific assessments for certain positions.

6. **Check References:**

- Contact previous employers or references to verify the candidate's work history and performance.

7. **Orientation:**

- Provide a comprehensive orientation for new hires, including an introduction to the restaurant's culture, values, and policies.

Training:

1. **Basic Training:**

- Conduct a general orientation covering the restaurant's layout, policies, and procedures.

- Provide an overview of the menu and service standards.

2. **Position-Specific Training:**

- Tailor training programs based on the specific needs of each role.

- For servers, focus on customer service, order-taking, and upselling techniques.

- For kitchen staff, emphasize food safety, preparation methods, and menu knowledge.

3. **Customer Service Training:**

- Train staff on effective communication, conflict resolution, and handling customer complaints.

- Emphasize the importance of creating a positive dining experience.

4. **Health and Safety Training:**

- Prioritize training on health and safety protocols, including food handling, sanitation, and emergency procedures.

- Ensure staff is aware of and complies with local health regulations.

5. **Continuous Training:**

   - Implement ongoing training programs to keep staff updated on new menu items, promotions, and industry trends.

   - Provide opportunities for cross-training to enhance versatility among team members.

6. **Team Building:**

   - Foster a sense of teamwork through team-building activities and regular staff meetings.

   - Encourage open communication and collaboration among team members.

7. **Performance Feedback:**

   - Establish a system for providing constructive feedback and performance reviews.

   - Recognize and reward outstanding performance to motivate the staff.

Remember, investing time and effort in hiring and training will contribute to a skilled, motivated, and cohesive team, ultimately enhancing the overall dining experience for your customers.

Chapter 26

Marketing and Promotion

Marketing and promotions are essential for the success of a restaurant. Here are some strategies you can implement to effectively market and promote your restaurant:

1. **Create an Online Presence:**

   - Develop a professional and user-friendly website with your menu, contact information, and high-quality images of your dishes.

   - Utilize social media platforms like Facebook, Instagram, Twitter, and Pinterest to engage with your audience. Share enticing food photos, behind-the-scenes glimpses, and customer testimonials.

2. **Social Media Marketing:**

   - Run targeted advertising campaigns on social media to reach your desired audience.

   - Host contests or giveaways to encourage user engagement and sharing.

   - Use relevant hashtags to increase the visibility of your posts.

3. **Online Reviews and Reputation Management:**

   - Encourage satisfied customers to leave positive reviews on popular review sites like Yelp, Google My Business, and TripAdvisor.

   - Respond promptly and professionally to both positive and negative reviews to show that you value customer feedback.

4. **Loyalty Programs:**

   - Implement a customer loyalty program to reward repeat customers. This could include discounts, free items, or exclusive access to special events.

5. **Email Marketing:**

- Build an email list of customers and send regular newsletters with updates, promotions, and special offers.

- Personalize emails based on customer preferences and behavior.

6. **Collaborations and Partnerships:**

- Partner with local businesses or influencers for joint promotions. This can help you tap into new audiences.

- Collaborate with food bloggers or influencers for reviews or features on their platforms.

7. **Events and Specials:**

- Host special events, theme nights, or live entertainment to create buzz and attract new customers.

- Introduce limited-time offers, seasonal menus, or discounts to encourage repeat visits.

8. **Search Engine Optimization (SEO):**

- Optimize your website and online content for search engines to improve your restaurant's visibility in search results.

- Use relevant keywords related to your cuisine, location, and specialties.

9. **Professional Photography:**

- Invest in high-quality, professional photographs of your dishes. Visual appeal is crucial in attracting customers, especially through online platforms.

10. **Community Involvement:**

- Participate in local events, sponsor local sports teams, or get involved in community fundraisers. This can enhance your restaurant's image and increase local support.

11. **Mobile Apps and Online Ordering:**

- Develop a mobile app or partner with popular food delivery apps to make your menu easily accessible to a wider audience.

Remember to track the effectiveness of your marketing strategies by analyzing data, such as customer feedback, online reviews, website traffic, and social media engagement. Adjust your approach based on the insights gained to continuously improve your restaurant's marketing efforts.

Chapter 27

Soft Opening

A soft opening is a pre-opening phase for a restaurant that allows the business to test its operations, service, and menu in a controlled environment before the official grand opening. It's an opportunity to identify and address any issues or areas for improvement before a larger public launch. Here are some key steps you might consider for a successful soft opening:

1. **Invite a Limited Audience:**

   - Limit the number of guests to ensure that the staff can manage the workload effectively.

   - Invite friends, family, and local influencers who can provide constructive feedback.

2. **Discounts and Special Offers:**

   - Offer special discounts or promotions during the soft opening to attract customers.

   - This can encourage people to try the restaurant and provide valuable feedback.

3. **Limited Menu:**

   - Consider starting with a simplified menu featuring a selection of your signature dishes.

   - This helps the kitchen staff get used to the workflow and allows for better quality control.

4. **Training Staff:**

   - Use the soft opening as a training ground for your staff.

   - This includes both the kitchen and front-of-house staff to ensure they are familiar with their roles and responsibilities.

5. **Gather Feedback:**
   - Create a feedback system for guests to share their experiences.
   - Encourage honest opinions on the food, service, ambiance, and overall dining experience.

6. **Fix Issues Promptly:**
   - Use the feedback received to identify and address any issues promptly.
   - This could include tweaking the menu, refining service processes, or making adjustments to the restaurant's layout.

7. **Social Media Engagement:**
   - Leverage social media platforms to generate buzz about the soft opening.
   - Encourage guests to share their experiences online, helping to create awareness and anticipation for the grand opening.

8. **Community Involvement:**
   - Connect with the local community by inviting neighbors and building relationships with nearby businesses.
   - Consider collaborating with local influencers or media to generate more publicity.

9. **Test Systems and Equipment:**
   - Ensure that all kitchen equipment, POS systems, and other operational elements are working smoothly.
   - Identify and address any technical issues during the soft opening phase.

10. **Pre-Grand Opening Event:**
    - Consider hosting a small event or gathering on the final day of the soft opening to thank the participants and build excitement for the grand opening.

Remember, the goal of a soft opening is to gather valuable insights, refine your processes, and create positive word-of-mouth before the official grand opening. It's an essential step in ensuring a successful launch and long-term success for your restaurant.

Chapter 28

Grand Opening

Grand openings are exciting events that can set the tone for the success of a restaurant. Here's a step-by-step guide on how to plan and execute a memorable grand opening for your restaurant:

Pre-Event Planning:

1. **Set a Date and Time:**

   - Choose a date and time that suits your target audience and local community.

   - Consider weekends or evenings when people are more likely to attend.

2. **Create a Budget:**

   - Determine the budget for the grand opening event, considering expenses like decorations, marketing, food, and entertainment.

3. **Permits and Licenses:**

   - Ensure that you have all the necessary permits and licenses for the event, especially if you plan to serve alcohol or have live entertainment.

4. **Invitations:**

   - Design and send out invitations well in advance, targeting local residents, influencers, and potential customers.

   - Leverage social media platforms to create buzz and invite a broader audience.

5. **Collaborate with Local Businesses:**

   - Partner with nearby businesses for cross-promotion. This can help expand your reach and bring in more attendees.

Event Day:

1. **Decorations:**
   - Create an inviting and thematic atmosphere that reflects your restaurant's identity.
   - Use banners, balloons, and signage to attract attention.

2. **Red Carpet Entrance:**
   - Make guests feel special with a red-carpet entrance and a warm welcome.

3. **Menu Sampling:**
   - Offer complimentary samples of your signature dishes to showcase your culinary offerings.

4. **Live Entertainment:**
   - Consider hiring local musicians, DJs, or performers to entertain the guests.

5. **Speeches and Ribbon Cutting:**
   - Plan a short speech to thank everyone for their support.
   - Include a ribbon-cutting ceremony with local dignitaries or influencers.

6. **Photography and Videography:**
   - Capture the moments professionally. Share the highlights on social media and your website.

7. **Contests and Giveaways:**
   - Organize contests or raffles with prizes to engage attendees and create excitement.

8. **Social Media Engagement:**
   - Encourage attendees to share their experiences on social media using a dedicated event hashtag.

Post-Event:

1. **Follow-Up:**

    - Send thank-you emails to attendees and express gratitude for their support.

2. **Promotions:**

    - Offer post-event promotions to keep the momentum going.

3. **Collect Feedback:**

    - Gather feedback from guests to identify areas for improvement.

4. **Publicize the Success:**

    - Share event highlights and photos on your website and social media platforms.

Remember, the key is to create a positive and memorable experience that leaves a lasting impression on your guests. A successful grand opening can generate ongoing interest and loyalty from the community.

Chapter 29

Monitor and Adjust

After the grand opening of a restaurant, it's crucial to monitor its operations and make adjustments as needed to ensure its success. Here are some key areas to focus on:

1. **Customer Feedback:**

   - Collect and analyse customer feedback through surveys, online reviews, and direct interactions.

   - Pay attention to both positive and negative comments to identify areas that require improvement or deserve recognition.

   - Act on feedback promptly to address any concerns or enhance positive aspects.

2. **Employee Performance:**

   - Evaluate the performance of your staff to ensure they are delivering high-quality service.

   - Provide additional training or support if necessary.

   - Encourage a positive work environment to boost employee morale and productivity.

3. **Menu Optimization:**

   - Analyze sales data to identify popular and unpopular menu items.

   - Consider introducing new dishes or modifying existing ones based on customer preferences.

   - Monitor food costs and adjust menu prices accordingly to maintain profitability.

4. **Operational Efficiency:**

   - Review and streamline operational processes to enhance efficiency.

- Evaluate inventory management to minimize waste and control costs.
- Ensure that the kitchen and serving staff are well-coordinated to provide timely service.

5. **Marketing Strategies:**
   - Assess the effectiveness of your marketing efforts.
   - Consider running promotions, discounts, or loyalty programs to attract and retain customers.
   - Explore new marketing channels or partnerships to reach a wider audience.

6. **Financial Analysis:**
   - Regularly review financial statements and assess the restaurant's overall financial health.
   - Adjust budgets and financial plans based on actual performance.
   - Monitor cash flow and make necessary adjustments to maintain financial stability.

7. **Ambiance and Atmosphere:**
   - Evaluate the ambiance and cleanliness of the restaurant.
   - Make adjustments to the decor or layout if needed.
   - Ensure that the overall atmosphere aligns with your target audience and concept.

8. **Technology Integration:**
   - Utilize technology for reservations, ordering, and payments to enhance customer experience.
   - Keep up with technological trends and adopt new tools that can improve efficiency.

9. **Community Engagement:**
   - Engage with the local community through events, sponsorships, or collaborations.

- Build a strong online presence through social media to connect with customers and promote your restaurant.

10. Legal Compliance:

- Ensure that the restaurant complies with all relevant health and safety regulations.

- Stay informed about changes in local laws and regulations affecting the restaurant industry.

Regularly reassessing and adapting your restaurant's operations based on feedback and performance metrics will contribute to its long-term success in a competitive market.

Part 5

Sustain

Chapter 30
Restaurant Business Challenges

Running a restaurant business comes with its own set of challenges. Sustaining and growing in the highly competitive food industry requires addressing various factors. Here are some common challenges faced by restaurant businesses:

1. **Intense Competition:** The restaurant industry is highly competitive, and new establishments constantly enter the market. Staying relevant and distinctive in a crowded space can be challenging.

2. **Changing Consumer Preferences:** Tastes and preferences of consumers evolve, and keeping up with these changes can be difficult. Regularly updating menus and adapting to new trends is crucial for staying appealing to customers.

3. **Labor Shortages:** Finding and retaining skilled kitchen and service staff is a persistent challenge. High turnover rates can disrupt operations and impact the quality of service.

4. **Operating Costs:** Managing expenses, including food costs, rent, utilities, and wages, is critical for profitability. Fluctuations in the cost of ingredients and other overheads can impact the bottom line.

5. **Health and Safety Compliance:** Restaurants need to adhere to strict health and safety regulations, especially in the post-pandemic era. Ensuring compliance can be demanding and requires ongoing efforts.

6. **Online Reviews and Reputation Management:** The rise of online review platforms means that a restaurant's reputation is constantly under scrutiny. Negative reviews can have a significant impact on business, and managing online presence is crucial.

7. **Technology Integration:** Keeping up with technology trends, including online ordering systems, reservation platforms, and

point-of-sale systems, is essential. Failure to adopt or integrate relevant technologies can put a restaurant at a disadvantage.

8. **Supply Chain Disruptions:** Dependence on a complex supply chain for fresh and quality ingredients can expose restaurants to risks. Disruptions due to weather, political events, or other factors can impact the availability and cost of essential items.

9. **Marketing and Branding:** Effectively promoting a restaurant and building a strong brand is an ongoing challenge. Marketing efforts need to be consistent and adapt to changing consumer behaviours.

10. **Economic Factors:** Economic downturns or uncertainties can affect consumers' dining-out habits. Restaurants need to be resilient to economic fluctuations and adapt their strategies accordingly.

11. **Sustainability Concerns:** Increasing awareness of environmental issues has led consumers to demand more sustainable practices. Restaurants need to consider eco-friendly options, from sourcing ingredients to managing waste.

12. **Crisis Management:** Unexpected events, such as natural disasters or public health crises (like the COVID-19 pandemic), can severely impact the restaurant industry. Having contingency plans in place is crucial for business

Chapter 31

Key Factors for Sustain Restaurant Business

Sustaining a restaurant business requires a combination of strategic planning, operational efficiency, marketing, and customer satisfaction. Here are some key factors to consider:

1. **Quality Food and Service:**

   - Ensure that the quality of your food and service consistently meets or exceeds customer expectations.

   - Train your staff to provide excellent customer service, as a positive dining experience often leads to repeat business and positive word-of-mouth.

2. **Unique Selling Proposition (USP):**

   - Differentiate your restaurant from competitors by offering a unique selling proposition. This could be a signature dish, a themed atmosphere, or any other factor that sets your restaurant apart.

3. **Adaptability and Innovation:**

   - Stay adaptable to changes in the market and consumer preferences. Innovate your menu, introduce new dishes, and be open to incorporating food trends to keep your offerings fresh and appealing.

4. **Marketing and Promotion:**

   - Develop a strong marketing strategy to create awareness about your restaurant. Utilize online and offline channels, including social media, to reach a broader audience.

   - Offer promotions, loyalty programs, and discounts to attract new customers and retain existing ones.

5. **Online Presence and Delivery Services:**

- Establish a strong online presence with a user-friendly website and active social media profiles.

- Consider partnering with food delivery services to expand your reach and cater to customers who prefer dining at home.

6. **Cost Control:**

- Monitor and control your operational costs effectively. This includes ingredients, labour, utilities, and other overhead expenses.

- Regularly review supplier contracts and negotiate better deals to maximize your profit margins.

7. **Customer Feedback and Improvement:**

- Encourage customer feedback and reviews. Use this information to identify areas for improvement and address any issues promptly.

- Constantly seek ways to enhance the overall customer experience based on constructive feedback.

8. **Employee Training and Morale:**

- Invest in training programs for your staff to ensure they are skilled and motivated.

- Maintain a positive work environment to boost employee morale, as satisfied employees are more likely to provide better service.

9. **Health and Safety Compliance:**

- Adhere to health and safety regulations and maintain high cleanliness standards to create a safe dining environment for customers.

10. **Financial Planning:**

- Develop a sound financial plan and budget. Regularly review financial statements and adjust your strategies as needed to ensure long-term sustainability.

11. Community Engagement:

- Build a strong connection with the local community. Participate in local events, sponsorships, or collaborate with neighbouring businesses to increase visibility and support.

By focusing on these aspects, you can create a solid foundation for your restaurant business and increase the likelihood of long-term success. Regularly reassess and adjust your strategies based on market trends and customer feedback.

Chapter 32

Sustainable Restaurant Business Practices

Quality Food and Service

Creating a restaurant that focuses on both quality food and sustainable practices requires careful planning and execution. Here are some key aspects to consider:

1. Sourcing of Ingredients:

- **Local and Organic:** Emphasize locally sourced and organic ingredients to support local farmers and reduce the carbon footprint associated with transportation.

- **Seasonal Menu:** Design a menu that reflects seasonal availability, ensuring freshness and sustainability.

2. Menu Planning:

- **Vegetarian and Vegan Options:** Include a variety of vegetarian and vegan options to cater to a broader range of dietary preferences and reduce the environmental impact of meat production.

- **Sustainable Seafood:** If you serve seafood, ensure it comes from sustainable and responsibly managed sources.

3. Waste Reduction:

- **Composting and Recycling:** Implement a comprehensive recycling and composting program to minimize waste sent to landfills.

- **Reduced Portion Sizes:** Offer reasonable portion sizes to minimize food waste and allow customers to order according to their appetite.

4. Energy Efficiency:

- **Energy-Efficient Appliances:** Invest in energy-efficient kitchen equipment and appliances to reduce energy consumption.

- **LED Lighting:** Use LED lighting to save energy and create a pleasant dining atmosphere.

5. Water Conservation:

- **Low-Flow Fixtures:** Install low-flow faucets and water-efficient dishwashing equipment to conserve water.

- **Water-Neutral Initiatives:** Consider initiatives like rainwater harvesting to reduce reliance on municipal water sources.

6. Sustainable Practices:

- **Biodegradable Packaging:** Use eco-friendly and biodegradable packaging materials to reduce the environmental impact of takeout orders.

- **Reusable Utensils and Plates:** If feasible, use reusable utensils, plates, and glassware instead of disposable options.

7. Community Engagement:

- **Education Programs:** Educate staff and customers about sustainability practices and the environmental impact of food choices.

- **Local Community Support:** Engage with the local community, support local initiatives, and participate in events that promote sustainability.

8. Ethical Labor Practices:

- **Fair Wages:** Ensure fair wages and ethical treatment of staff to promote a positive work environment.

- **Training Programs:** Provide training programs for staff on sustainable practices and the importance of their role in maintaining them.

9. Certifications and Recognition:

- **Green Certifications:** Obtain certifications from recognized sustainability organizations to showcase your commitment to eco-friendly practices.

- **Transparency:** Clearly communicate your sustainability efforts to customers through menus, websites, or promotional materials.

10. Continuous Improvement:

- **Regular Audits:** Conduct regular audits to assess the effectiveness of your sustainability initiatives and identify areas for improvement.

- **Adaptability:** Stay informed about new sustainable practices and be willing to adapt your restaurant's operations accordingly.

By combining quality food with sustainable practices, you not only contribute to the well-being of the environment but also appeal to a growing market of conscientious consumers.

Chapter 33

Unique Selling Proposition (USP)

Unique Selling Proposition (USP):

A Unique Selling Proposition (USP) is a distinctive factor or feature that sets a product, service, or business apart from its competitors in the eyes of customers. For a restaurant, having a strong USP can be crucial in attracting and retaining customers. Here are some potential USPs that a restaurant might consider:

1. **Cuisine and Specialization:**

   - Offering a unique or specialized cuisine that is not readily available in the area.

   - Providing a fusion of different culinary styles for a unique dining experience.

2. **Signature Dishes or Chef Specials:**

   - Highlighting specific dishes that are exclusive to the restaurant and are known for their exceptional taste or presentation.

3. **Health and Dietary Focus:**

   - Emphasizing a commitment to health-conscious menu options, catering to specific dietary needs (e.g., vegan, gluten-free), or using locally-sourced, organic ingredients.

4. **Ambiance and Theme:**

   - Creating a distinctive atmosphere or theme that enhances the dining experience, making it memorable for customers.

5. **Innovative Culinary Techniques:**

   - Incorporating unique cooking methods, molecular gastronomy, or other innovative culinary techniques to distinguish the restaurant from competitors.

6. **Entertainment or Interactive Elements:**

   - Offering live entertainment, themed events, or interactive dining experiences to engage customers beyond just the food.

7. **Exceptional Service:**

   - Providing top-notch customer service, personalized attention, or unique service features that go beyond what is commonly expected.

8. **Ethical and Sustainable Practices:**

   - Emphasizing ethical sourcing, sustainable practices, or involvement in community initiatives to appeal to socially conscious consumers.

9. **Exclusive Membership or Loyalty Programs:**

   - Introducing special membership programs, loyalty rewards, or VIP privileges for regular customers.

10. **Convenience and Technology:**

   - Incorporating advanced technology, such as online ordering, innovative payment methods, or interactive menus, to enhance the overall dining experience.

It's essential for a restaurant to thoroughly understand its target market and tailor its USP to align with the preferences and needs of its customers. The goal is to offer something that competitors do not, creating a compelling reason for customers to choose your restaurant over others.

Chapter 34

Adaptability and Innovation

Adaptability and Innovation

Adaptability and innovation are crucial for the sustainability of restaurants, especially during the sustain phase where the goal is to maintain success and continue thriving in a competitive market. Here are some strategies for incorporating adaptability and innovation in the sustain phase of restaurants:

1. **Menu Innovation:**

   - Regularly update the menu to keep it fresh and exciting for customers.

   - Introduce seasonal dishes or special limited-time offerings to create a sense of urgency and encourage repeat visits.

2. **Technology Integration:**

   - Embrace technology for online ordering, reservations, and payments to enhance customer convenience.

   - Consider implementing smart kitchen systems to improve efficiency and reduce waste.

3. **Sustainability Practices:**

   - Adopt sustainable and locally sourced ingredients to appeal to environmentally conscious customers.

   - Implement eco-friendly practices such as minimizing food waste and using recyclable packaging.

4. **Flexible Business Models:**

   - Explore different business models, such as a hybrid approach with dine-in, takeout, and delivery services.

- Consider pop-up events, collaborations, or catering services to diversify revenue streams.

5. **Customer Feedback and Data Analysis:**

   - Regularly gather feedback from customers through surveys or social media to identify areas for improvement.

   - Analyze customer data to understand preferences and tailor offerings accordingly.

6. **Employee Training and Development:**

   - Invest in ongoing training for staff to keep them updated on industry trends, customer service, and new culinary techniques.

   - Foster a culture of innovation by encouraging employees to contribute ideas and suggestions.

7. **Collaborations and Partnerships:**

   - Collaborate with local businesses or chefs for special events or promotions.

   - Partner with food delivery services to expand your reach and customer base.

8. **Marketing Strategies:**

   - Utilize social media platforms to showcase new dishes, promotions, and behind-the-scenes content.

   - Implement loyalty programs and discounts to encourage repeat business.

9. **Adaptable Space Design:**

   - Design the restaurant space to be flexible, allowing for easy reconfiguration for different events or themes.

   - Create multi-functional spaces that can be used for private events, workshops, or entertainment.

10. **Health and Wellness Focus:**

    - Offer healthier menu options to cater to health-conscious customers.

- Highlight nutritional information on the menu to meet the growing demand for transparency.

11. Crisis Preparedness:

- Develop contingency plans for unforeseen challenges, such as economic downturns or public health crises.

- Stay informed about industry trends and be prepared to pivot quickly if necessary.

By embracing adaptability and innovation, restaurants can stay relevant, meet evolving customer expectations, and navigate the challenges of the sustain phase more effectively.

Chapter 35

Online Presence and Delivery services

Creating a strong online presence and utilizing delivery services are crucial aspects for businesses in the modern digital landscape. Here are some key points to consider:

Online Presence:

1. **Website:**

   - **Responsive Design:** Ensure your website is mobile-friendly and works well on various devices.

   - **User-Friendly Interface:** Make it easy for visitors to navigate and find information.

   - **E-commerce Integration:** If applicable, incorporate an e-commerce platform for online transactions.

2. **Social Media:**

   - **Choose Relevant Platforms:** Be present on platforms where your target audience is active.

   - **Consistent Branding:** Maintain a cohesive brand image across all social media channels.

   - **Engagement:** Interact with your audience through comments, messages, and posts.

3. **Search Engine Optimization (SEO):**

   - **Keyword Optimization:** Use relevant keywords in your website content for better search engine visibility.

   - **Quality Content:** Regularly update your website with high-quality, relevant content.

   - **Backlinks:** Build backlinks from reputable sources to improve your website's authority.

4. **Online Advertising:**

- **Google Ads:** Utilize Google Ads to increase visibility in search engine results.

- **Social Media Ads:** Invest in targeted ads on platforms like Facebook, Instagram, or Twitter.

5. **Email Marketing:**

- **Build a Subscriber List:** Encourage website visitors to subscribe to newsletters.

- **Personalization:** Tailor your email campaigns based on customer preferences and behavior.

Delivery Services:

1. **Delivery Platforms:**

- **Third-Party Delivery Services:** Partner with established platforms like Uber Eats, DoorDash, or Grubhub.

- **In-House Delivery:** Consider developing your own delivery infrastructure for more control.

2. **Online Ordering System:**

- **Mobile Apps:** Create a user-friendly mobile app for easy ordering.

- **Website Ordering:** Allow customers to place orders directly through your website.

3. **Efficient Logistics:**

- **Real-time Tracking:** Provide customers with the ability to track their orders in real-time.

- **Optimized Routes:** Optimize delivery routes to minimize delivery times and costs.

4. **Customer Communication:**

- **Confirmation Messages:** Send order confirmation messages and estimated delivery times.

- **Feedback Collection:** Encourage customers to provide feedback on their delivery experience.

5. **Promotions and Loyalty Programs:**

   - **Discounts:** Offer promotions or discounts for online orders.

   - **Loyalty Programs:** Implement programs to reward repeat customers.

6. **Health and Safety Measures:**

   - **Contactless Delivery:** Provide options for contactless delivery.

   - **Transparent Communication:** Clearly communicate any safety measures implemented in response to health concerns.

Remember to regularly update and adapt your strategies based on customer feedback, technological advancements, and changes in the business landscape.

Chapter 36

Cost Control

Cost control is crucial for the successful operation of a restaurant. Here are some key areas to focus on to effectively manage and control costs in a restaurant:

1. **Menu Planning:**

    - Regularly analyse the cost and profitability of each menu item.

    - Consider the popularity of dishes and their contribution to overall sales.

    - Adjust menu prices to reflect changes in ingredient costs.

2. **Inventory Management:**

    - Implement a strict inventory control system to track all incoming and outgoing goods.

    - Use a First-In-First-Out (FIFO) method to minimize waste and spoilage.

    - Negotiate with suppliers for bulk discounts and better deals.

3. **Supplier Relationships:**

    - Establish good relationships with reliable suppliers.

    - Negotiate favorable terms, discounts, and payment terms.

    - Explore options for local sourcing to reduce transportation costs.

4. **Staff Training and Management:**

    - Train staff on proper portion control and food handling to minimize waste.

    - Schedule employees efficiently to match demand, preventing overstaffing.

- Implement cross-training to ensure staff can handle various roles.

5. **Energy Efficiency:**
   - Optimize energy use by using energy-efficient equipment and appliances.
   - Regularly maintain and clean kitchen equipment to ensure efficiency.
   - Turn off unnecessary lights and equipment during non-peak hours.

6. **Technology and Automation:**
   - Implement point-of-sale (POS) systems to track sales and inventory in real-time.
   - Use technology for online ordering, reservations, and delivery services.
   - Automate repetitive tasks to reduce labor costs.

7. **Waste Management:**
   - Monitor and minimize food wastage by accurately forecasting demand.
   - Implement recycling programs to reduce waste disposal costs.
   - Consider composting organic waste.

8. **Menu Engineering:**
   - Highlight high-profit margin items on the menu.
   - Encourage upselling of high-margin items to increase revenue.
   - Regularly review and update the menu based on profitability analysis.

9. **Regular Financial Analysis:**
   - Conduct regular financial reviews to identify trends and areas for improvement.
   - Compare actual costs to budgeted costs and adjust accordingly.
   - Utilize accounting software to streamline financial processes.

10. Customer Feedback:

- Collect and analyse customer feedback to identify areas for improvement.

- Use feedback to enhance the overall dining experience and customer satisfaction.

- Satisfied customers are likely to return, reducing the cost of acquiring new customers.

By consistently monitoring and managing these aspects, a restaurant can improve its cost control measures and enhance overall financial performance. Regularly reassessing and adapting strategies based on changing market conditions and customer preferences is also crucial for long-term success.

Chapter 37
Customer Feedback and Improvement

In the sustain phase of a restaurant business, customer feedback plays a crucial role in identifying areas for improvement and maintaining a positive customer experience. Here are some strategies and considerations for managing customer feedback and driving improvements during this phase:

1. **Implement a Feedback System:**

    - Establish a systematic approach for collecting customer feedback. This could include comment cards, online surveys, or feedback forms on your website.

    - Encourage customers to provide feedback through various channels, such as social media, review sites, and direct communication.

2. **Monitor Online Reviews:**

    - Regularly monitor online review platforms like Yelp, Google Reviews, and TripAdvisor to stay informed about customer sentiments.

    - Respond promptly and professionally to both positive and negative reviews. Addressing negative feedback publicly demonstrates a commitment to customer satisfaction.

3. **Train Staff for Customer Interaction:**

    - Ensure that your staff is trained to solicit feedback from customers during their dining experience. This can be done through friendly conversations or discreet surveys.

    - Train staff on how to handle negative feedback, turning it into an opportunity to resolve issues and show your commitment to customer satisfaction.

4. **Use Technology for Feedback:**

   - Implement digital solutions like mobile apps or QR codes on tables that allow customers to provide feedback easily.

   - Leverage technology to analyse and organize feedback data efficiently, identifying trends and patterns.

5. **Regularly Review Feedback Data:**

   - Schedule regular reviews of customer feedback data to identify common themes or recurring issues.

   - Prioritize the feedback based on its impact on customer satisfaction and operational efficiency.

6. **Customer Feedback Meetings:**

   - Conduct regular meetings to discuss customer feedback with key staff members. This collaborative approach can lead to innovative solutions and shared responsibility for improvement.

   - Celebrate successes and improvements as a team, fostering a positive and proactive work environment.

7. **Implement Continuous Improvement Initiatives:**

   - Develop action plans based on feedback to address specific issues or areas for improvement.

   - Regularly reassess and adjust strategies based on ongoing feedback and changes in customer expectations.

8. **Sustainability Practices:**

   - If your restaurant emphasizes sustainability, seek feedback on your eco-friendly initiatives and make adjustments based on customer suggestions.

   - Communicate your commitment to sustainability and how customer feedback contributes to your ongoing efforts.

9. **Community Engagement:**

   - Engage with the local community to gather feedback on your restaurant's role and impact.

- Support local causes or events based on community input, enhancing your brand's reputation.

10. Celebrate Customer Loyalty:

- Recognize and reward loyal customers. Implement a loyalty program that offers incentives for repeat business and encourages ongoing feedback.

By actively seeking and acting on customer feedback, your restaurant can continuously evolve to meet the changing needs and expectations of your patrons, contributing to long-term success in the sustain phase.

Chapter 38

Employee Training and Morale

In the sustain phase of a restaurant business, employee training and morale remain crucial for ensuring continued success and maintaining a positive work environment. Here are some key considerations for managing employee training and morale during this phase:

Employee Training:

1. **Ongoing Training Programs:**

   - Implement continuous training programs to keep employees updated on new menu items, service standards, and industry trends.

   - Provide cross-training opportunities to help employees understand different roles within the restaurant, enhancing their skills and versatility.

2. **Technology Integration:**

   - If the restaurant adopts new technologies or software, ensure employees receive adequate training to use these tools efficiently. This could include point-of-sale systems, reservation software, or kitchen management systems.

3. **Food Safety and Compliance:**

   - Regularly reinforce food safety protocols and compliance standards. Conduct periodic training sessions to ensure that employees are well-versed in health and safety regulations.

4. **Customer Service Training:**

   - Focus on customer service training to maintain a high level of hospitality. Emphasize the importance of positive interactions with customers, handling complaints effectively, and creating memorable dining experiences.

5. **Team Building:**

    - Facilitate team-building activities to strengthen interpersonal relationships among staff. This can improve communication, collaboration, and overall morale within the workplace.

Employee Morale:

1. **Recognition and Rewards:**

    - Recognize and reward employees for their hard work and dedication. This can include employee of the month awards, performance bonuses, or other incentives to boost morale.

2. **Open Communication:**

    - Foster open communication between management and staff. Regularly solicit feedback from employees and address any concerns or suggestions they may have. This helps in making them feel valued and heard.

3. **Work-Life Balance:**

    - Promote a healthy work-life balance by scheduling reasonable working hours and offering flexibility when possible. This can contribute to employee satisfaction and well-being.

4. **Career Development Opportunities:**

    - Provide opportunities for career growth and advancement within the organization. This could include promotions, additional responsibilities, or access to further training and education.

5. **Employee Wellness Programs:**

    - Implement wellness programs to support the physical and mental well-being of employees. This can include fitness classes, counseling services, or initiatives that promote a healthy lifestyle.

6. **Celebrate Milestones:**

    - Acknowledge and celebrate employee milestones such as work anniversaries. This reinforces a sense of belonging and loyalty among staff members.

7. **Flexibility and Adaptability:**

- Demonstrate flexibility and adaptability in response to changing circumstances. This shows that the management is responsive to the needs of its employees and the evolving industry.

By investing in ongoing training and maintaining high morale, a restaurant can ensure that its staff remains engaged, motivated, and well-equipped to contribute to the sustained success of the business.

Chapter 39

Health and Safety Compliance

The sustain phase of a restaurant business involves maintaining and improving health and safety compliance to ensure the well-being of both employees and customers. Here are key considerations for sustaining health and safety compliance in a restaurant:

1. **Regular Training and Education:**

    - Conduct regular training sessions for staff on health and safety protocols, including food handling, sanitation, and emergency procedures.

    - Keep employees informed about updates in health and safety regulations and guidelines.

2. **Documented Policies and Procedures:**

    - Ensure that all health and safety policies and procedures are well-documented and easily accessible to staff.

    - Regularly review and update these documents to reflect any changes in regulations or best practices.

3. **Inspections and Audits:**

    - Conduct regular health and safety inspections to identify and address any potential hazards or compliance issues.

    - Keep records of inspections and audits, and use them to make improvements to your safety protocols.

4. **Hygiene Practices:**

    - Emphasize the importance of personal hygiene among staff, including handwashing, proper use of gloves, and the use of hairnets or caps.

- Implement a robust cleaning schedule for all areas of the restaurant, including kitchen equipment, dining areas, and restrooms.

5. **Food Safety Management:**

- Implement and maintain a Hazard Analysis and Critical Control Points (HACCP) plan to identify and control food safety hazards.

- Regularly monitor and record food temperatures, and ensure that all staff are trained in safe food handling practices.

6. **Emergency Preparedness:**

- Have a well-defined emergency response plan in place for events such as fires, power outages, or natural disasters.

- Conduct regular drills to ensure that staff are familiar with emergency procedures.

7. **Communication and Reporting:**

- Establish clear channels of communication for reporting safety concerns or incidents.

- Encourage open communication between staff and management to address potential issues promptly.

8. **Regulatory Compliance:**

- Stay informed about changes in local health and safety regulations and adjust your practices accordingly.

- Maintain all necessary licenses and permits, and renew them on time.

9. **Wellness Programs:**

- Implement wellness programs to promote the health and well-being of employees, reducing the risk of illness and absenteeism.

10. **Customer Communication:**

- Communicate your commitment to health and safety to customers through signage, menus, and online platforms.

- Solicit feedback from customers to identify areas for improvement.

By focusing on these aspects, a restaurant can sustain a high level of health and safety compliance, ensuring a safe and enjoyable experience for both employees and customers. Regular monitoring, training, and adjustments to protocols based on feedback and changing regulations are crucial elements of this phase.

Chapter 40

Community Engagement

Community Engagement

In the sustain phase of a restaurant business, community engagement becomes crucial for long-term success. Sustaining a restaurant involves maintaining a loyal customer base, fostering positive relationships, and contributing to the local community. Here are some strategies for community engagement in the sustain phase of a restaurant business:

1. **Local Partnerships:**

   - Collaborate with local businesses, suppliers, and farmers to source ingredients locally. This not only supports the community but also provides fresh and unique offerings for your menu.

   - Partner with nearby businesses for joint promotions or events to cross-promote each other and attract a broader audience.

2. **Community Events:**

   - Host events and activities within the restaurant or sponsor local community events. This could include charity fundraisers, cultural celebrations, or even hosting local art exhibitions.

   - Organize themed nights or special events that resonate with the local community's interests.

3. **Sustainability Initiatives:**

   - Implement sustainable practices in your restaurant, such as reducing waste, recycling, and using eco-friendly packaging. Communicate these initiatives to customers to demonstrate your commitment to environmental responsibility.

   - Educate the community on your sustainable practices and encourage them to adopt similar behaviors.

4. **Customer Loyalty Programs:**

- Establish loyalty programs that reward repeat customers. Offer discounts, special promotions, or exclusive events for loyal patrons to make them feel appreciated.

- Use social media and email marketing to communicate directly with your customer base, updating them on upcoming events, promotions, or changes in the menu.

5. **Feedback and Involvement:**

- Encourage customer feedback and actively respond to reviews, both positive and negative. Show customers that their opinions matter and that you are committed to continuous improvement.

- Involve the community in decision-making processes, such as voting on new menu items or providing input on potential changes to the restaurant.

6. **Community Outreach Programs:**

- Engage in local philanthropy or charitable activities. This could involve sponsoring local sports teams, contributing to community development projects, or supporting educational initiatives.

- Actively participate in community service and encourage your staff to get involved as well.

7. **Social Media Presence:**

- Maintain an active presence on social media platforms to engage with the community online. Share behind-the-scenes content, customer stories, and updates about the restaurant.

- Run social media campaigns or contests that involve the community, encouraging user-generated content and interaction.

8. **Customer Appreciation Events:**

- Host events specifically to show appreciation to your customers. This could include customer appreciation nights with special discounts, complimentary items, or exclusive access to new menu items.

By actively engaging with the local community through partnerships, events, sustainability initiatives, loyalty programs, feedback mechanisms, and outreach programs, your restaurant can build a strong and loyal customer base, contributing to the sustained success of your business.

Chapter 41
Financial Planning

Financial planning is crucial for the sustained success of a restaurant business. In the sustain phase, the focus is on maintaining profitability, optimizing operations, and ensuring long-term viability. Here are key aspects of financial planning in the sustain phase of the restaurant business:

1. **Budgeting and Forecasting:**

   - Develop a comprehensive budget that includes all operational expenses, such as rent, utilities, labour, and food costs.

   - Use forecasting tools to predict future revenue based on historical data, market trends, and seasonality.

2. **Cost Control:**

   - Regularly review and analyse costs, especially food and labour costs, to identify areas for optimization.

   - Implement cost-saving measures without compromising the quality of products or services.

3. **Menu Engineering:**

   - Evaluate the profitability of each menu item and focus on promoting high-margin items.

   - Consider redesigning the menu to highlight popular and profitable dishes.

4. **Marketing Strategies:**

   - Develop cost-effective marketing strategies to maintain and grow customer engagement.

   - Leverage social media, loyalty programs, and partnerships to attract and retain customers.

5. **Technology Integration:**

   - Implement technology solutions such as point-of-sale (POS) systems and inventory management software to streamline operations and reduce human errors.

   - Explore online ordering and delivery platforms to reach a broader audience.

6. **Employee Training and Retention:**

   - Invest in ongoing training for staff to enhance efficiency and customer service.

   - Implement retention strategies to reduce turnover, as hiring and training new employees can be costly.

7. **Customer Experience:**

   - Focus on delivering an exceptional customer experience to encourage repeat business and positive word-of-mouth.

   - Collect feedback and adapt your services based on customer preferences.

8. **Debt Management:**

   - If applicable, manage any existing debts effectively, and avoid taking on unnecessary debt.

   - Negotiate favourable terms with suppliers and creditors to improve cash flow.

9. **Diversification and Expansion:**

   - Explore opportunities for diversification, such as catering services, partnerships, or new menu offerings.

   - Consider expansion cautiously, ensuring that existing operations are stable before taking on additional risks.

10. **Regular Financial Analysis:**

   - Conduct regular financial analyses to monitor key performance indicators (KPIs) and identify any deviations from the financial plan.

- Adjust strategies based on performance data to ensure financial goals are met.

11. Emergency Fund:

- Maintain a financial buffer or emergency fund to handle unforeseen circumstances, such as economic downturns or unexpected expenses.

By implementing these financial planning strategies, a restaurant can increase its resilience and navigate challenges while ensuring sustained profitability and growth. Regularly reassess and adjust your financial plan to adapt to changing market conditions.

The worldwide food business is supposed to ascend to $4.2 trillion by 2024.

This has seen many restaurant owners try to scale their businesses. However, success in the food service industry is not easy, and about 60% of restaurants fail in their first year. The biggest mistake most owners make is scaling their business just for the sake of growing it, without knowing how they will sustain the growth. In addition, most restaurants fail to scale up successfully as they do not plan adequately or choose the right location to set up their new business

Multiple Ways to grow your Restaurant Business and scale new heights

Chapter 42

Creating A Successful Restaurant Brand

Creating a successful restaurant brand involves a combination of thoughtful planning, creativity, and strategic execution. Here's a step-by-step guide to help you build your restaurant brand:

1. **Define Your Concept:**

   - Clearly articulate the concept of your restaurant. What type of cuisine will you offer? What is the ambiance like? What makes your restaurant unique?

2. **Identify Your Target Audience:**

   - Understand your target market. Who are your ideal customers? Consider demographics, preferences, and lifestyle.

3. **Create a Unique Selling Proposition (USP):**

   - Determine what sets your restaurant apart from others. It could be a signature dish, a unique atmosphere, or exceptional service.

4. **Choose a Memorable Name:**

   - Select a name that is easy to remember, reflects your brand personality, and is not easily confused with other businesses.

5. **Design an Attractive Logo and Branding Elements:**

   - Invest in professional branding that reflects your restaurant's identity. This includes a well-designed logo, colour scheme, and other visual elements.

6. **Develop a Consistent Brand Voice:**

   - Define the tone and personality of your brand. Whether it's casual, formal, playful, or sophisticated, maintain a consistent voice across all communication channels.

7. **Create a Strong Online Presence:**

   - Establish a user-friendly website with high-quality images of your food and restaurant. Leverage social media platforms to engage with your audience and showcase your brand.

8. **Craft a Menu that Reflects Your Brand:**

   - Design a menu that aligns with your brand concept and caters to your target audience. Consider unique dishes, presentation, and pricing.

9. **Train and Empower Your Staff:**

   - Your staff is an integral part of your brand. Ensure they understand the brand values and can deliver a consistent experience to customers.

10. **Focus on Customer Experience:**

    - Provide exceptional customer service. The overall experience should reflect your brand promise, from the moment customers enter your restaurant to the time they leave.

11. **Utilize Marketing Strategies:**

    - Develop marketing campaigns to promote your restaurant. This could include online and offline strategies, such as social media advertising, partnerships, and special events.

12. **Collect and Respond to Feedback:**

    - Encourage customer feedback and actively respond to reviews. This not only helps in improving your services but also shows that you value customer opinions.

13. **Build Community Engagement:**

    - Engage with your local community. Sponsor events, collaborate with other businesses, and participate in local activities to strengthen your brand presence.

14. **Adapt and Evolve:**

    - Stay responsive to market trends and customer preferences. Regularly revisit and, if necessary, update your brand strategy to remain relevant.

15. Monitor and Measure Success:

- Establish key performance indicators (KPIs) to measure the success of your branding efforts. Monitor customer satisfaction, online reviews, and other relevant metrics.

Building a restaurant brand is an ongoing process that requires dedication, consistency, and a genuine connection with your customers. Regularly assess and adjust your strategies to ensure long-term success.

Part 6

Scale Up

Chapter 43

Location

The positioning or location of a restaurant is crucial during the scale-up phase as it can significantly impact the success of the business. Here are some considerations for positioning and location:

1. **Target Audience and Demographics:**

   - Identify your target audience and their demographics. Understand their preferences, behaviours, and lifestyles. Choose a location that aligns with your target market.

2. **Competitor Analysis:**

   - Research and analyse the competition in the chosen location. Look for gaps in the market or areas where your restaurant can offer something unique.

3. **Foot Traffic and Accessibility:**

   - Choose a location with high foot traffic to increase visibility and attract potential customers. Ensure that the restaurant is easily accessible by public transportation and has ample parking if needed.

4. **Local Community and Culture:**

   - Consider the local community and culture. Tailor your restaurant concept and menu to fit the preferences and tastes of the community. Engage with local events and build relationships with nearby businesses.

5. **Economic Factors:**

   - Evaluate the economic factors of the area, such as income levels and spending habits. Ensure that the pricing of your restaurant aligns with the economic profile of the target market.

6. **Zoning and Regulations:**

   - Check local zoning regulations and legal requirements for restaurants in the chosen location. Ensure that you comply with all necessary permits and health codes.

7. **Technology and Online Presence:**

   - Leverage technology to enhance your online presence. Ensure that your restaurant is visible on popular food delivery platforms and that your online presence is optimized for search engines.

8. **Scalability and Expansion Plans:**

   - Consider the scalability of the location. If you plan to expand further, choose a location that allows for scalability and growth without major logistical challenges.

9. **Collaboration and Partnerships:**

   - Explore collaborations with nearby businesses or establishments that complement your restaurant. This can enhance your marketing efforts and create a synergistic effect.

10. **Customer Feedback and Adaptability:**

    - Stay adaptable and open to customer feedback. Regularly assess the performance of your restaurant in the chosen location and be willing to make changes if necessary.

Remember that the right positioning and location can contribute significantly to the success of your restaurant during the scale-up phase. Regularly reassess the market conditions and make adjustments to your strategy as needed.

Chapter 44

Supply Chain

The supply chain is a critical component of the restaurant business, and managing it efficiently becomes even more crucial during the scale-up of operations. Here are key aspects to consider when scaling up a restaurant business:

1. **Vendor Relationships:**

    - Strengthen existing relationships and negotiate favourable terms with suppliers.

    - Consider diversifying suppliers to mitigate risks associated with dependence on a single source.

    - Regularly review vendor performance and seek continuous improvement.

2. **Inventory Management:**

    - Implement robust inventory management systems to track stock levels, reduce waste, and prevent overordering.

    - Utilize technology, such as point-of-sale (POS) systems, to automate inventory tracking and ordering processes.

    - Forecast demand accurately to optimize inventory levels and avoid stockouts or excess stock.

3. **Distribution and Logistics:**

    - Evaluate and optimize the logistics of your supply chain to ensure timely deliveries and minimize transportation costs.

    - Consider centralizing distribution to streamline operations and reduce overhead.

    - Implement efficient routing and delivery scheduling to improve overall logistics.

4. **Quality Control:**

   - Set quality standards for ingredients and products and communicate them clearly to suppliers.

   - Conduct regular quality inspections to ensure consistency across multiple locations.

   - Implement feedback loops with suppliers to address quality issues promptly.

5. **Scalable Processes:**

   - Standardize processes to ensure consistency across all locations.

   - Invest in scalable technology solutions such as inventory management software, order processing systems, and POS systems.

   - Streamline kitchen processes to handle increased order volumes efficiently.

6. **Demand Planning:**

   - Analyze historical sales data to predict future demand accurately.

   - Collaborate with suppliers to adjust orders based on seasonal fluctuations or promotional events.

   - Implement data-driven decision-making to optimize the supply chain for changing demand patterns.

7. **Cost Management:**

   - Continuously evaluate and negotiate pricing with suppliers to ensure competitiveness.

   - Implement cost-saving measures, such as bulk purchasing, to benefit from economies of scale.

   - Regularly review and optimize all aspects of the supply chain to identify areas for cost reduction.

8. **Regulatory Compliance:**

   - Stay informed about food safety regulations and compliance requirements in all locations.

- Ensure that suppliers adhere to quality and safety standards.

- Implement traceability systems to quickly identify and respond to any potential food safety issues.

9. **Training and Communication:**

- Provide comprehensive training for staff on new processes and technologies.

- Establish clear communication channels with suppliers, distributors, and internal teams to address issues promptly.

- Foster a culture of collaboration and continuous improvement.

10. **Adaptability:**

- Stay agile and be prepared to adjust your supply chain strategy based on market trends and business needs.

- Regularly reassess and optimize your supply chain in response to changing customer preferences and industry dynamics.

By carefully managing these aspects, a restaurant business can successfully scale up while maintaining operational efficiency, quality standards, and cost-effectiveness in its supply chain.

Chapter 45

Networking

Scaling up a restaurant business involves expanding its operations, reach, and efficiency. Networking plays a crucial role in this process, as it helps you connect with various stakeholders, build partnerships, and leverage resources. Here are several aspects of networking that can contribute to the scale-up of a restaurant business:

1. **Supplier Relationships:**

   - **Local Sourcing:** Establish relationships with local suppliers for fresh and quality ingredients. This can lead to better pricing, consistent supply, and potentially unique offerings.

   - **Negotiation Skills:** Develop strong negotiation skills to secure favourable terms with suppliers. This may include bulk purchasing or special discounts for long-term partnerships.

2. **Collaborations and Partnerships:**

   - **Delivery Platforms:** Partner with popular food delivery platforms to expand your reach without the need for significant infrastructure investments.

   - **Catering Services:** Collaborate with event planners or corporate clients for catering opportunities, providing an additional revenue stream.

   - **Cross-Promotions:** Partner with other local businesses for cross-promotional opportunities, helping both parties reach new customers.

3. **Digital Marketing and Social Media:**

   - **Online Presence:** Leverage social media platforms to create an online presence and engage with customers. Utilize targeted digital marketing strategies to attract a larger audience.

- **Influencer Collaborations:** Partner with local influencers or bloggers to create awareness and generate buzz around your restaurant.

4. **Community Engagement:**

   - **Local Events:** Participate in or host local events to connect with the community. This can enhance brand visibility and build a loyal customer base.

   - **Sponsorship:** Sponsor local sports teams, charities, or community events to strengthen your ties with the community.

5. **Technology Integration:**

   - **Point of Sale (POS) Systems:** Implement efficient POS systems to streamline operations, track sales, and manage inventory.

   - **Customer Relationship Management (CRM):** Utilize CRM systems to maintain customer data, preferences, and feedback, enabling personalized services and targeted marketing.

6. **Training and Development:**

   - **Staff Networking:** Encourage networking among your staff to share best practices and learn from each other.

   - **Training Programs:** Develop training programs for employees to enhance their skills, ensuring a consistently high level of service as you expand.

7. **Investor and Funding Networks:**

   - **Pitch to Investors:** If seeking funding for expansion, network with potential investors or venture capitalists who specialize in the restaurant industry.

   - **Government Programs:** Explore government programs or grants that support small businesses and restaurants.

8. **Professional Associations:**

   - **Join Associations:** Become a member of local and national restaurant associations to access resources, industry insights, and networking opportunities.

Remember, effective networking is not just about making connections but also about building and nurturing relationships. This can lead to valuable collaborations, increased brand visibility, and enhanced operational efficiency, all of which are crucial for successfully scaling up a restaurant business.

Chapter 46

Process & Systems

Scaling up a restaurant business involves expanding its operations, increasing its capacity, and ensuring efficient processes. Here are some key aspects of business processes and systems to consider for scaling up a restaurant:

1. **Standardized Operations:**

   - Document and standardize your recipes, cooking processes, and presentation standards to maintain consistency across all locations.

   - Implement standardized training programs for staff to ensure that everyone follows the same procedures and maintains the same level of quality.

2. **Technology Integration:**

   - Implement a Point of Sale (POS) system that can handle multiple locations and provide real-time reporting.

   - Use kitchen management systems to streamline order processing and kitchen communication.

   - Invest in online ordering and delivery platforms to reach a broader customer base.

3. **Supply Chain Management:**

   - Establish strong relationships with suppliers and negotiate bulk purchasing agreements to ensure consistent and cost-effective supply of ingredients.

   - Implement inventory management systems to track stock levels, reduce waste, and optimize ordering.

4. **Employee Management:**

- Develop clear organizational structures and job roles to support the increased workload.

- Implement human resource management systems to handle payroll, employee scheduling, and performance tracking.

- Offer training and development programs to help employees adapt to changes and acquire new skills.

5. **Customer Relationship Management (CRM):**

- Utilize CRM systems to track customer preferences and feedback across all locations.

- Implement loyalty programs and promotional activities to retain existing customers and attract new ones.

6. **Quality Control:**

- Implement quality control measures to ensure that the food and service maintain the same standard as you scale.

- Regularly conduct audits and inspections to identify and address any issues promptly.

7. **Legal and Compliance:**

- Ensure that all locations comply with local health and safety regulations, licensing requirements, and other legal obligations.

- Establish a legal and compliance team or work with external experts to navigate legal complexities associated with expansion.

8. **Financial Management:**

- Implement robust financial management systems to monitor expenses, revenue, and profits for each location.

- Conduct regular financial audits to identify areas for improvement and cost-saving.

9. **Marketing and Branding:**

- Develop a strong brand identity and marketing strategy to maintain a consistent image across all locations.

- Utilize digital marketing, social media, and local advertising to promote new locations and attract customers.

10. Scalable Infrastructure:

- Choose scalable technologies and infrastructure that can grow with your business.
- Consider cloud-based solutions for scalability and flexibility.

11. Feedback Mechanisms:

- Establish a system for collecting and analyzing feedback from customers and employees to continuously improve processes and address issues.

Remember, successful scaling requires careful planning, effective execution, and the ability to adapt to changing circumstances. Regularly assess and adjust your strategies as needed to ensure sustained growth and success.

Chapter 47
Collaborations

Collaborations can be instrumental in scaling up a restaurant business. Here are several potential collaboration opportunities to consider:

1. **Partnerships with Food Delivery Platforms:**

    - Collaborate with popular food delivery platforms to expand your reach and cater to a wider audience. This allows you to tap into their existing customer base and leverage their delivery infrastructure.

2. **Joint Marketing Initiatives:**

    - Partner with local businesses or influencers for joint marketing campaigns. This could involve cross-promotions, where both parties promote each other's products or services to their respective audiences.

3. **Catering Collaborations:**

    - Collaborate with event planners, wedding coordinators, or businesses that frequently require catering services. Offering your restaurant's catering services can be a lucrative way to scale up.

4. **Collaborative Menu Items:**

    - Partner with other local businesses to create collaborative menu items. For example, team up with a local bakery for a dessert collaboration. This can attract new customers from both businesses.

5. **Loyalty Program Alliances:**

    - Form alliances with other businesses to create a shared loyalty program. Customers can earn points or discounts that can be redeemed at any of the collaborating businesses, fostering customer loyalty.

6. **Technology Integration:**

   - Collaborate with technology providers to integrate advanced POS systems, online ordering platforms, or reservation systems. This can enhance the overall customer experience and streamline operations.

7. **Cross-Promotions with Complementary Businesses:**

   - Identify businesses that complement yours, such as a wine shop, coffee shop, or dessert shop. Cross-promote each other's offerings to encourage customers to visit both establishments.

8. **Collaborative Events:**

   - Host collaborative events with other local businesses. This could include food festivals, wine tastings, or themed nights. Collaborative events can draw larger crowds and create a buzz in the community.

9. **Community Sponsorships:**

   - Sponsor local events or sports teams. This not only contributes to community development but also enhances your restaurant's visibility and reputation.

10. **Franchising or Licensing:**

    - Explore franchising or licensing opportunities to replicate your restaurant's success in new locations. This allows others to operate under your brand while you benefit from their success.

11. **Supplier Collaborations:**

    - Negotiate with local suppliers for bulk discounts or exclusive deals. Collaborating with suppliers can help reduce costs and improve overall operational efficiency.

12. **Collaborative Training Programs:**

    - Collaborate with culinary schools or training programs to offer internships or hands-on training for aspiring chefs. This can be a source of skilled manpower for your restaurant.

Remember to thoroughly assess potential collaborators, ensuring that their values align with yours and that the collaboration brings mutual benefits. Regularly evaluate the effectiveness of collaborations to make adjustments as needed for optimal results.

Chapter 48

Expansion Plan For Local, Regional, National And International

Expanding a restaurant business on different scales, from local to international, requires careful planning and execution. Here's a general framework for each level of expansion:

Local Expansion:

1. **Market Research:**

   - Identify local market trends and consumer preferences.

   - Assess competition and find a unique selling proposition.

2. **Operational Efficiency:**

   - Streamline operations to handle increased demand.

   - Ensure consistency in food quality and service.

3. **Marketing:**

   - Use local advertising channels such as community events, social media, and local publications.

   - Leverage loyalty programs and discounts for repeat customers.

4. **Collaborations:**

   - Partner with local businesses for cross-promotions.

   - Establish relationships with local suppliers for fresh ingredients.

5. **Customer Feedback:**

   - Collect and analyze feedback to make necessary improvements.

   - Engage with the local community through events and promotions.

Regional Expansion:

1. **Feasibility Study:**

   - Conduct a comprehensive study of potential regions for expansion.
   - Consider factors like demographics, economic conditions, and cultural preferences.

2. **Brand Consistency:**

   - Standardize processes to maintain the brand's identity.
   - Implement a robust training program for staff.

3. **Supply Chain Management:**

   - Strengthen relationships with suppliers and distributors.
   - Optimize the supply chain for efficient regional distribution.

4. **Technology Integration:**

   - Implement technology solutions for centralized management of multiple locations.
   - Consider online ordering systems and mobile apps.

5. **Marketing Campaigns:**

   - Develop region-specific marketing campaigns.
   - Utilize digital marketing for broader reach.

National Expansion:

1. **Legal and Regulatory Compliance:**

   - Understand and comply with national regulations.
   - Adjust business practices as per national standards.

2. **Brand Adaptation:**

   - Customize the menu or marketing strategies based on national preferences.
   - Consider regional variations in cultural tastes.

3. **Logistics and Distribution:**
   - Build a robust logistics network for nationwide supply chain.
   - Establish central kitchens for consistency.

4. **Scale Up Infrastructure:**
   - Invest in scalable technology and infrastructure.
   - Consider franchise models for faster expansion.

5. **Public Relations:**
   - Engage in national PR campaigns to build brand awareness.
   - Collaborate with influencers and celebrities for wider reach.

International Expansion:

1. **Cultural Sensitivity:**
   - Understand and respect cultural nuances in target markets.
   - Adapt menus and marketing strategies accordingly.

2. **Legal and Compliance:**
   - Navigate international legal and regulatory requirements.
   - Establish partnerships with local experts.

3. **Localization:**
   - Customize offerings to suit local tastes and preferences.
   - Translate marketing materials and menus appropriately.

4. **Global Supply Chain:**
   - Develop a global supply chain to ensure consistency.
   - Establish international partnerships for sourcing ingredients.

5. **Brand Image:**
   - Maintain a consistent global brand image.
   - Utilize international PR and marketing strategies.

Remember to continually monitor and adapt your strategies based on market feedback and changing conditions. Each level of expansion requires a deep understanding of the local market and a flexible approach to accommodate diverse consumer preferences.

Chapter 49

Funding For Scaling Up

Funding for scaling up a restaurant business can come from various sources. Here are some common options to consider:

1. **Traditional Bank Loans:**

   - Approach local banks or financial institutions to secure a business loan. You'll need a solid business plan, financial projections, and collateral.

2. **Small Business Administration (SBA) Loans or MSME loans:**

   - The SBA offers various loan programs to help small businesses. These loans often come with favourable terms and lower interest rates.

3. **Investors:**

   - Seek out investors who are interested in the restaurant industry. This could include angel investors, venture capitalists, or private equity firms.

4. **Crowdfunding:**

   - Platforms like Kickstarter or Indiegogo allow you to raise funds from a large number of people who believe in your business concept. This is particularly effective if you have a unique and compelling story.

5. **Friends and Family:**

   - Approach friends and family members who may be willing to invest in your business. Clearly outline the terms of the investment to avoid misunderstandings.

6. **Government Grants:**

   - Some government agencies offer grants or subsidies to small businesses, especially those in specific industries or locations. Research local and federal grant opportunities.

7. **Franchising:**

    - If your restaurant concept is easily replicable, you might consider franchising. Franchisees typically contribute funds to open additional locations.

8. **Equipment Financing:**

    - If you need funding specifically for new equipment, consider equipment financing. This allows you to borrow money to purchase equipment and repay the loan over time.

9. **Business Lines of Credit:**

    - A business line of credit provides flexible access to funds that you can use for various business purposes, including scaling up your restaurant.

10. **Alternative Lenders:**

    - Explore alternative lending options, such as online lenders or peer-to-peer lending platforms. These often have quicker approval processes but may come with higher interest rates.

11. **Grants and Competitions:**

    - Some organizations or institutions host grants or business competitions for entrepreneurs. Winning such competitions can provide both funding and exposure.

Before seeking funding, it's crucial to have a clear business plan that outlines your expansion strategy, financial projections, and how the funds will be utilized. Additionally, be prepared to demonstrate the viability and potential success of your restaurant business to potential investors or lenders.

Chapter 50

Initial Public Offering (IPO) Journey

The Initial Public Offering (IPO) journey for businesses is a complex process that involves several stages and careful planning. Going public through an IPO allows a private company to raise capital by selling shares to the public for the first time.

Taking a restaurant business public through an Initial Public Offering (IPO) can be a complex and multifaceted process. Here's a general overview of the steps involved in the IPO journey for scaling up a restaurant business:

1. **Preparation and Evaluation:**

   - **Financial Readiness:** Ensure that your financials are in order. Audited financial statements are often required for IPOs.

   - **Business Model Evaluation:** Assess the scalability and sustainability of your restaurant business model.

   - **Legal and Regulatory Compliance:** Ensure compliance with all relevant regulations and legal requirements.

2. **Engage Professional Advisors:**

   - **Legal Counsel:** Hire legal advisors to navigate the complex legal requirements associated with going public.

   - **Financial Advisors:** Engage financial advisors who specialize in IPOs to guide you through the process.

   - **Underwriters:** Select underwriters to manage the IPO process and help with the sale of shares.

3. **Financial Preparation:**

   - **Financial Statements:** Prepare audited financial statements that comply with regulatory standards.

   - **Valuation:** Determine the valuation of your restaurant business, which will influence the IPO pricing.

4. **Due Diligence:**

- **Internal Due Diligence:** Conduct a thorough internal review of your operations, finances, and legal compliance.

- **External Due Diligence:** Allow external parties, including underwriters and regulatory bodies, to perform due diligence.

5. **Registration and Filing:**

- **File with Regulatory Bodies:** Submit the necessary documents to regulatory bodies, such as the Securities and Exchange Commission (SEC) in the United States.

- **Prospectus Development:** Create a prospectus that provides detailed information about your restaurant business for potential investors.

6. **Roadshow:**

- **Investor Presentations:** Conduct a roadshow to present your restaurant business to potential investors and generate interest.

- **Meetings with Institutional Investors:** Engage in one-on-one meetings with institutional investors to address their questions and concerns.

7. **Pricing and Allocation:**

- **Set IPO Price:** Work with underwriters to determine the IPO price per share.

- **Allocate Shares:** Decide how shares will be allocated among institutional and retail investors.

8. **IPO Launch:**

- **Stock Exchange Listing:** List your restaurant business on a stock exchange.

- **Public Offering:** Open the IPO for public subscription, allowing investors to purchase shares.

9. **Post-IPO Compliance:**

- **Continuous Disclosure:** Comply with ongoing disclosure requirements and financial reporting standards.

- **Shareholder Relations:** Establish effective communication channels with shareholders to build trust and transparency.

10. Operational Expansion:

- **Utilize IPO Funds:** Use the capital raised from the IPO to scale up operations, expand the restaurant chain, and invest in marketing and technology.

It's essential to note that the IPO process can vary based on jurisdiction and regulatory requirements. Consulting with financial and legal experts experienced in IPOs is crucial to navigate the complexities of going public successfully.

Part 7

Financials

Chapter 51

Cost Components

The restaurant business involves various costs that contribute to its overall operation. These costs can be categorized into several major components:

1. **Startup Costs:**

   - **Location and Lease:** Expenses related to finding and securing a suitable location for the restaurant, including lease payments and any necessary renovations or build-outs.

   - **Licenses and Permits:** Costs associated with obtaining the required licenses and permits to operate a restaurant legally.

   - **Equipment and Furnishings:** Purchasing or leasing kitchen equipment, dining furniture, POS systems, and other necessary items.

2. **Operational Costs:**

   - **Labor Costs:** Wages, salaries, and benefits for staff, including chefs, cooks, servers, bartenders, and cleaning staff.

   - **Food and Beverage Costs:** Expenses related to purchasing and maintaining an inventory of food and beverages. This includes raw ingredients, beverages, and any pre-packaged items.

   - **Utilities:** Costs for electricity, water, gas, and other essential services.

   - **Insurance:** Insurance premiums to cover various risks, including property, liability, and worker's compensation.

   - **Marketing and Advertising:** Expenditures on marketing campaigns, advertising, promotions, and public relations efforts to attract customers.

- **Technology:** Costs associated with point-of-sale systems, reservation systems, and other technological tools to streamline operations.

- **Cleaning and Maintenance:** Expenses for cleaning supplies, equipment maintenance, and repairs.

- **Waste Management:** Costs related to waste disposal and recycling.

3. **Overhead Costs:**

- **Rent:** Ongoing payments for leasing the restaurant space.

- **Loan Repayments:** If the restaurant has taken out loans for startup or expansion, regular repayments are part of the overhead costs.

- **Property Taxes:** Taxes levied on the restaurant property.

- **Depreciation:** Accounting for the decrease in value of assets over time.

4. **Administrative Costs:**

- **Accounting and Legal Fees:** Expenses for professional services related to accounting, bookkeeping, and legal compliance.

- **Office Supplies:** Costs for paper, ink, pens, and other office necessities.

- **Software and Technology:** Expenses for software subscriptions and technology tools used for administrative purposes.

5. **Contingency and Miscellaneous Costs:**

- **Contingency Fund:** Setting aside funds for unexpected expenses or emergencies.

- **Training:** Costs associated with staff training and development programs.

- **Contests and Promotions:** Budget for running special promotions, discounts, or contests to attract customers.

Understanding and managing these cost components is crucial for the financial health and sustainability of a restaurant business. Careful budgeting, monitoring, and cost control measures are essential for long-term success.

Chapter 52
Capital Expenditure (CapEx) Budget

Creating a capital expenditure (CapEx) budget for a restaurant involves estimating and planning for significant, long-term expenses related to assets and improvements. Here are some common items to consider when developing a CapEx budget for a restaurant:

1. **Kitchen Equipment:**
   - Commercial-grade stoves, ovens, refrigerators, and freezers.
   - Industrial dishwashers and other kitchen appliances.

2. **Interior Furnishings:**
   - Tables, chairs, and booths.
   - Lighting fixtures.
   - Decorative elements.

3. **Technology:**
   - Point of Sale (POS) systems.
   - Reservation systems.
   - Kitchen display systems.

4. **Renovations and Remodeling:**
   - Structural improvements.
   - Flooring, painting, and wall coverings.
   - Restroom upgrades.

5. **Exterior Improvements:**
   - Outdoor seating areas.
   - Signage and landscaping.

6. **HVAC Systems:**

- Heating, ventilation, and air conditioning systems.

7. **Security Systems:**

- Surveillance cameras.

- Alarm systems.

8. **Vehicles:**

- Delivery vehicles.

- Catering vans.

9. **Training and Development:**

- Employee training programs.

- Staff development initiatives.

10. **License and Permit Fees:**

- Costs associated with obtaining and renewing licenses.

11. **Franchise Fees (if applicable):**

- Payments to the franchisor for brand use.

12. **Reserve Fund:**

- A contingency fund for unexpected expenses.

When creating the CapEx budget, consider the lifespan of each asset and plan for replacements or upgrades accordingly. Additionally, account for any ongoing maintenance costs associated with the new assets.

It's crucial to regularly review and update the Capex budget to reflect changes in the business environment, technology, and industry trends. A well-structured Capex budget can help ensure that the restaurant maintains and improves its infrastructure over time, contributing to its long-term success.

Chapter 53

Working Capital

For a restaurant to manage its working capital effectively, it's essential to:

1. **Monitor Cash Flow:** Regularly track cash inflows and outflows.

2. **Efficient Inventory Management:** Minimize excess inventory to avoid tying up too much capital.

3. **Negotiate Favourable Terms:** Negotiate with suppliers for favourable payment terms to manage accounts payable.

4. **Improve Accounts Receivable:** Encourage prompt payments from customers to improve cash inflow.

5. **Plan for Seasonal Fluctuations:** Restaurants often experience seasonal variations, and planning for these fluctuations is crucial.

It's important to note that the specific factors affecting working capital can vary based on the size of the restaurant, its business model, and the local market conditions. Regular financial analysis and adjustments to operational strategies are key to maintaining a healthy working capital position in the restaurant industry.

Chapter 54

Cashflow Tracking

The cash flow of a restaurant business is a crucial aspect of its financial management, reflecting the movement of money into and out of the business over a specific period. Effective cash flow management is essential for the sustainability and success of any restaurant. Here's a breakdown of key components and considerations for understanding and managing the cash flow of a restaurant:

1. **Revenue Sources:**

   - **Sales:** The primary source of cash inflow for a restaurant is its sales. This includes revenue from food and beverage sales, catering services, and any other income-generating activities.

2. **Operating Expenses:**

   - **Cost of Goods Sold (COGS):** This includes the direct costs associated with producing the food and beverages, such as ingredients and raw materials.

   - **Labor Costs:** Salaries and wages for kitchen staff, servers, and other employees.

   - **Overhead Expenses:** Rent, utilities, insurance, maintenance, and other fixed and variable costs associated with running the restaurant.

3. **Non-operating Expenses:**

   - **Interest and Loan Repayments:** If the restaurant has borrowed money, interest and principal repayments need to be factored into the cash flow.

   - **Taxes:** Income taxes, sales taxes, and any other applicable taxes.

4. **Cash Inflow:**

   - **Customer Payments:** Cash received from customers through various payment methods, including cash, credit cards, and digital payments.

   - **Gift Cards and Vouchers:** Consider how these are accounted for when issued and redeemed.

5. **Cash Outflow:**

   - **Supplier Payments:** Payments to food and beverage suppliers.

   - **Employee Payments:** Wages, salaries, benefits, and any other compensation for employees.

   - **Operational Expenses:** Rent, utilities, insurance, and other day-to-day expenses.

   - **Loan Repayments:** If applicable, payments for loans or lines of credit.

6. **Timing Considerations:**

   - Restaurant businesses often face seasonality and fluctuations in customer demand. Understanding and planning for these variations is crucial for managing cash flow.

7. **Inventory Management:**

   - Effective inventory control helps optimize the use of resources and minimizes waste, positively impacting cash flow.

8. **Contingency Planning:**

   - Maintain a cash reserve for unforeseen circumstances or emergencies, such as equipment breakdowns, renovations, or unexpected drops in sales.

9. **Cash Flow Statement:**

   - Regularly review and update a cash flow statement, which outlines the inflows and outflows of cash over a specific period. This statement helps identify trends, potential issues, and areas for improvement.

10. Technology and Point of Sale (POS) Systems:

- Utilize modern POS systems that integrate with accounting software to streamline financial processes and provide real-time insights into cash flow.

Regular monitoring and proactive management of these factors are essential for maintaining a healthy cash flow in a restaurant business. Implementing sound financial practices and adapting to changes in the business environment can contribute to long-term success.

Chapter 55

Menu Pricing

Menu pricing is a crucial aspect of running a successful restaurant or any food-related business. Effective pricing strategies can contribute to profitability, customer satisfaction, and overall business success. Here are some common menu pricing strategies:

1. **Cost-Plus Pricing:**

   - Calculate the cost of each menu item, including ingredients, labour, and overhead.
   - Add a predetermined percentage markup to cover profit margin.
   - This straightforward method ensures that all costs are covered and provides a consistent profit margin.

2. **Competitive Pricing:**

   - Research competitors' prices for similar menu items.
   - Set your prices in line with or slightly below the market average.
   - This strategy helps attract price-sensitive customers and stay competitive in the market.

3. **Value-Based Pricing:**

   - Focus on the perceived value of your menu items.
   - Price items based on the value customers place on them rather than the cost.
   - Emphasize unique features, high-quality ingredients, or special preparation methods to justify higher prices.

4. **Psychological Pricing:**

   - Set prices just below a round number (e.g., $9.99 instead of $10.00).

- Use charm pricing to make prices appear more attractive to customers.

- This strategy can influence customer perceptions and increase sales.

5. **Bundle Pricing:**

   - Group related items together and offer them as a package at a discounted price.

   - Encourages customers to buy more and can increase overall revenue.

6. **Menu Engineering:**

   - Analyze the popularity and profitability of each menu item.

   - Place high-profit items strategically on the menu to encourage more sales.

   - Adjust pricing or promote items to maximize profitability.

7. **Dynamic Pricing:**

   - Adjust prices based on factors like demand, time of day, or season.

   - Common in the hospitality industry, dynamic pricing allows businesses to maximize revenue during peak times.

8. **Economic Order Quantity (EOQ):**

   - Calculate the optimal order quantity for ingredients to minimize costs.

   - This strategy helps in reducing overall expenses, which can be reflected in menu pricing.

9. **Tiered Pricing:**

   - Offer different versions of a product or service at varying price points.

   - For example, a small, medium, and large size with corresponding prices.

10. Seasonal Pricing:

- Adjust prices based on seasonal availability and demand.

- Offer seasonal specials or discounts to attract customers during specific times of the year.

11. Penetration Pricing:

- Introduce new items at lower initial prices to gain market share quickly.

- Prices may be increased later once the product gains popularity.

Consider the target market, location, and positioning of your restaurant when selecting a pricing strategy. It's often effective to combine multiple strategies and regularly review pricing based on market conditions and customer feedback.

Chapter 56

The Daily Sales And Cost Report

[Restaurant Name]

Daily Sales and Cost Report

Date: [Date]

Sales:

- Total Sales: $___________
- Food Sales: $___________
- Beverage Sales: $___________

Costs:

- Cost of Goods Sold (COGS):
- Food Cost: $___________
- Beverage Cost: $___________
- Total COGS: $___________
- Operating Expenses:
- Labor Cost: $___________
- Rent: $___________
- Utilities: $___________
- Marketing/Advertising: $___________
- Other Operating Expenses: $___________
- Total Operating Expenses: $___________
- Total Costs: $___________

Profit/Loss:

- Gross Profit: $___________ (Total Sales - Total COGS)

- Net Profit: $____________ (Gross Profit - Total Operating Expenses)

Key Performance Indicators:

- Gross Profit Margin: _______% (Gross Profit / Total Sales * 100)
- Net Profit Margin: _______% (Net Profit / Total Sales * 100)
- Food Cost Percentage: _______% (Food Cost / Food Sales * 100)
- Beverage Cost Percentage: _______% (Beverage Cost / Beverage Sales * 100)

Sales Breakdown:

- Number of Customers: ____________
- Average Transaction Value: $____________ (Total Sales / Number of Customers)

Menu Performance:

- Best-Selling Item: ________________ (Name and quantity sold)
- Worst-Selling Item: ________________ (Name and quantity sold)

Notes:

- Any significant events or observations affecting sales or costs.

Recommendations:

- Suggestions for improving profitability or reducing costs.

Part 8

Go-Digital

Chapter 57

Digital Transformation

The digital transformation of restaurants involves leveraging technology to enhance various aspects of the restaurant business, from operations and customer service to marketing and management. Here are several key areas where digital transformation is making a significant impact in the restaurant industry:

1. **Online Ordering and Delivery Platforms:**

   - **Mobile Apps and Websites:** Restaurants are developing their own mobile apps and user-friendly websites to enable customers to place orders online.

   - **Third-Party Delivery Services:** Collaboration with popular third-party delivery platforms allows restaurants to reach a broader customer base.

2. **Digital Menus:**

   - **QR Code Menus:** Many restaurants are replacing traditional paper menus with QR code menus that customers can scan with their smartphones.

   - **Interactive Digital Menus:** Some establishments use tablets or digital screens to display dynamic and interactive menus.

3. **Table Reservation Systems:**

   - **Online Reservation Platforms:** Digital reservation systems help customers book tables in advance, reducing waiting times and enhancing the overall dining experience.

4. **Contactless Payments:**

   - **Mobile Wallets and Apps:** Contactless payment options, such as mobile wallets and apps, provide a secure and convenient way for customers to pay for their meals.

5. **Customer Relationship Management (CRM):**

   - **Data Analytics:** Restaurants use data analytics to understand customer preferences, track trends, and personalize marketing efforts.

   - **Loyalty Programs:** Digital loyalty programs and reward systems encourage repeat business and customer retention.

6. **Kitchen Management Systems:**

   - **Inventory Management:** Digital tools help manage inventory, reducing waste and ensuring that popular items are always in stock.

   - **Order Tracking Systems:** Streamlining kitchen processes with digital systems can enhance order accuracy and speed.

7. **Digital Marketing:**

   - **Social Media Presence:** Restaurants leverage social media platforms to engage with customers, promote specials, and build brand awareness.

   - **Online Advertising:** Targeted online advertising helps restaurants reach specific demographics and promote events or new menu items.

8. **Smart Technologies:**

   - **IoT Devices:** Internet of Things (IoT) devices like smart kitchen appliances can improve efficiency and automate certain tasks.

   - **Smart POS Systems:** Point-of-sale systems with advanced features facilitate smoother transactions and help manage various aspects of the business.

9. **Data Security and Compliance:**

   - **Secure Payment Processing:** Ensuring the security of customer payment information is crucial in the digital era.

   - **Compliance with Regulations:** Restaurants need to stay compliant with data protection and privacy regulations.

10. Staff Training and Management:

- **eLearning Platforms:** Digital platforms can be used for staff training, ensuring that employees stay updated on industry trends, hygiene practices, and customer service skills.

The digital transformation of restaurants is an ongoing process, and establishments that embrace technology can gain a competitive edge by providing a seamless and innovative dining experience for their customers.

Chapter 58

Cybersecurity

Cybersecurity is crucial in the restaurant business to protect sensitive customer information, financial transactions, and the overall integrity of the business. Here are key aspects to consider:

1. Protecting Customer Data

- **Encryption:** Use SSL/TLS encryption for online transactions and customer data storage.

- **Data Minimization:** Only collect the necessary customer information to reduce the risk if data is compromised.

2. Payment Security

- **PCI DSS Compliance:** Ensure that all payment systems comply with the Payment Card Industry Data Security Standard.

- **Tokenization:** Implement tokenization to replace sensitive card information with non-sensitive tokens during transactions.

3. Employee Training

- **Security Awareness:** Train employees on recognizing phishing attempts, proper handling of sensitive information, and secure password practices.

- **Access Control:** Limit access to sensitive systems and data to only those employees who need it.

4. Network Security

- **Secure Wi-Fi:** Use WPA3 encryption for your Wi-Fi network and keep customer and business networks separate.

- **Firewall and VPN:** Implement a strong firewall and use VPNs for secure remote access.

5. Regular Software Updates

- **Patch Management:** Regularly update all software, including POS systems, to protect against vulnerabilities.

- **Endpoint Protection:** Use antivirus and anti-malware tools to protect all devices connected to your network.

6. Third-Party Vendor Management

- **Vendor Security:** Ensure that third-party vendors, such as payment processors, adhere to strict cybersecurity standards.

- **Contracts and Agreements:** Have clear agreements that outline security expectations and responsibilities.

7. Incident Response Plan

- **Preparedness:** Develop an incident response plan to quickly address data breaches or cyber attacks.

- **Regular Drills:** Conduct regular drills to ensure that staff knows how to respond to a cybersecurity incident.

8. Customer Communication

- **Transparency:** Communicate openly with customers about how their data is protected.

- **Notification:** Have a plan in place for notifying customers if their data is compromised.

9. Cybersecurity Insurance

- **Risk Mitigation:** Consider investing in cybersecurity insurance to mitigate financial losses in the event of a data breach.

Implementing these cybersecurity measures can help safeguard your restaurant business from cyber threats and ensure the trust and safety of your customers

Appendix

Appendix A
Institutional Catering

Institutional catering refers to the provision of food services in various institutions such as schools, hospitals, businesses, government offices, and other organizations. This type of catering involves preparing and serving meals on a large scale to meet the specific needs of a particular institution and its patrons. Institutional catering may be provided by in-house catering teams or outsourced to external catering companies.

Key features of institutional catering include:

1. **Volume and Scale:** Institutional catering typically involves serving large quantities of food to accommodate the needs of a significant number of people. This requires efficient planning, preparation, and execution of meals.

2. **Nutritional Considerations:** Institutions often have specific dietary requirements and nutritional guidelines that must be followed. For example, schools may need to provide balanced and healthy meals for students, while hospitals may need to cater to patients with specific medical conditions.

3. **Menu Planning:** Institutional caterers must design menus that are diverse, appealing, and meet the dietary needs of their clientele. Menus may need to rotate regularly to ensure variety and prevent menu fatigue.

4. **Regulatory Compliance:** Institutional catering is subject to various health and safety regulations, and caterers must adhere to these standards to ensure the well-being of the individuals they are serving.

5. **Special Dietary Requirements:** Institutions may need to accommodate special dietary requirements, such as vegetarian or vegan options, food allergies, and cultural or religious considerations.

6. **Logistics and Distribution:** Efficient logistics are crucial in institutional catering to ensure that meals are delivered to the right locations at the right times. This may involve transportation, storage, and distribution considerations.

7. **Cost Control:** Given the scale of institutional catering, cost control is essential. Caterers must find a balance between providing quality meals and managing costs effectively.

Examples of institutional catering include:

- **School Cafeterias:** Providing meals for students and staff in educational institutions.

- **Hospital Catering:** Preparing and delivering meals for patients, healthcare professionals, and support staff in hospitals.

- **Corporate Cafeterias:** Offering food services to employees in large office buildings or business campuses.

- **Prison Catering:** Providing meals for inmates in correctional facilities.

- **Government Office Cafeterias:** Offering catering services to government employees working in various offices.

Institutional catering plays a crucial role in ensuring that individuals in different settings have access to nutritious and well-prepared meals that meet their specific needs.

Cross-cultural fusion

Cross-cultural fusion plays a significant role in the restaurant business, contributing to the diversity and innovation within the culinary landscape. Here are several ways in which cross-cultural fusion impacts the restaurant industry:

1. **Diverse Culinary Offerings:**
   - Cross-cultural fusion allows restaurants to combine elements from different culinary traditions, resulting in unique and diverse menu offerings.

- Restaurants can blend flavours, ingredients, and cooking techniques from various cultures, providing customers with a broader range of dining experiences.

2. **Innovation and Creativity:**

- Fusion cuisine encourages chefs to experiment and think creatively, leading to the development of new and innovative dishes.

- The combination of diverse culinary elements sparks creativity, pushing chefs to explore new flavor combinations and presentation styles.

3. **Appeal to a Broad Customer Base:**

- Offering a fusion of different cultures' cuisines helps attract a more diverse customer base.

- Restaurants can cater to customers with varied preferences, making it possible for individuals with different cultural backgrounds to find something they enjoy.

4. **Cultural Exchange and Understanding:**

- Cross-cultural fusion in restaurants facilitates cultural exchange and understanding among customers.

- It provides an opportunity for people to explore and appreciate different cultures through their culinary traditions.

5. **Global Trends and Influences:**

- Restaurants often draw inspiration from global culinary trends, incorporating popular ingredients, cooking techniques, and dishes from different parts of the world.

- Cross-cultural fusion allows restaurants to stay current with evolving tastes and preferences.

6. **Collaborations and Partnerships:**

- Collaboration between chefs from different cultural backgrounds can result in exciting fusion dishes and contribute to a sense of unity within the culinary community.

- Restaurants may collaborate with local farmers and suppliers from diverse backgrounds to source unique and authentic ingredients.

7. **Marketing and Branding Opportunities:**

   - A restaurant that successfully incorporates cross-cultural fusion can differentiate itself in the market and attract attention through unique branding.

   - Effective marketing strategies highlighting the fusion concept can create buzz and draw customers seeking novel dining experiences.

8. **Adaptation to Dietary Preferences:**

   - Cross-cultural fusion allows restaurants to adapt dishes to meet various dietary preferences and restrictions, such as vegetarian, vegan, gluten-free, or other dietary requirements.

9. **Tourist Appeal:**

   - In regions with diverse cultural influences, cross-cultural fusion can enhance a restaurant's appeal to tourists seeking an authentic and diverse culinary experience.

In summary, cross-cultural fusion plays a vital role in the restaurant business by fostering innovation, attracting a diverse customer base, promoting cultural exchange, and contributing to the dynamic and evolving nature of the culinary landscape.

Appendix B
Key Performance Indicators (KPIs)

Key Performance Indicators (KPIs) are crucial metrics that help assess the performance and success of a business. In the restaurant industry, several KPIs can be monitored to evaluate various aspects of operations. Here are some common KPIs for the restaurant industry:

1. **Sales and Revenue:**

    - Total Sales: The overall revenue generated by the restaurant.

    - Average Check: The average amount spent by a customer per visit.

    - Sales Growth: Percentage increase in sales compared to a previous period.

2. **Customer Satisfaction:**

    - Customer Feedback and Reviews: Positive reviews, ratings, and feedback from customers.

    - Net Promoter Score (NPS): A metric indicating customer loyalty and likelihood to recommend the restaurant.

3. **Table Turnover:**

    - Table Turnover Rate: The number of times a table is cleared and reset in a given time period, indicating the efficiency of service.

4. **Occupancy Rate:**

    - Dining Room Occupancy: The percentage of seating capacity filled during operating hours.

5. **Food Cost and Inventory Management:**

    - Food Cost Percentage: The percentage of total revenue spent on food costs.

- Inventory Turnover: The rate at which restaurant inventory is used or sold.

6. **Labor Cost:**

   - Labor Cost Percentage: The percentage of total revenue spent on labor (including salaries, benefits, and taxes).

   - Employee Turnover: The rate at which staff leaves and is replaced.

7. **Menu Performance:**

   - Popular Items: Identifying and tracking the most ordered menu items.

   - Profitability by Dish: Assessing the profitability of each menu item.

8. **Marketing Effectiveness:**

   - Return on Investment (ROI): Assessing the success of marketing campaigns in attracting customers.

   - Customer Acquisition Cost (CAC): The cost of acquiring a new customer.

9. **Reservation and Waitlist Metrics:**

   - Reservation Rate: Percentage of occupied tables reserved in advance.

   - Average Wait Time: The average time customers spend waiting for a table.

10. **Online Presence:**

    - Website and Social Media Engagement: Tracking website visits, social media likes, shares, and comments.

    - Online Order Volume: The number and value of online orders.

11. **Health and Safety Compliance:**

    - Health Inspection Scores: Compliance with health and safety regulations.

    - Employee Training: Monitoring staff training on food safety and hygiene.

12. Waste Management:

- Food Waste Percentage: The percentage of food that goes to waste compared to total inventory.

- Recycling and Sustainability Metrics: Assessing the restaurant's environmental impact.

These KPIs can vary based on the specific goals and focus areas of a restaurant. Regular monitoring and analysis of these metrics can help restaurant owners and managers make informed decisions to improve overall performance and profitability

Appendix C
Labour Management

Labour management in a restaurant is crucial for the efficient operation of the business. It involves various aspects, including staffing, scheduling, training, performance management, and compliance with labour laws. Here are some key considerations for effective labour management in a restaurant:

1. **Staffing:**

    - **Right Sizing:** Ensure that you have the appropriate number of staff based on the size of your restaurant, the volume of customers, and peak hours.

    - **Skill Levels:** Match staff skills to the specific roles they perform. This helps in maximizing efficiency and customer satisfaction.

2. **Scheduling:**

    - **Flexible Scheduling:** Create flexible schedules that align with peak business hours. Utilize scheduling software to optimize staff allocation during busy periods.

    - **Predictive Scheduling:** Anticipate busy periods and plan accordingly to avoid overstaffing or understaffing.

3. **Training:**

    - **Continuous Training:** Regularly train your staff to ensure they are up-to-date on menu items, service standards, and any new procedures.

    - **Cross-Training:** Cross-train employees so they can handle multiple roles, providing flexibility during busy times.

4. **Performance Management:**

    - **Performance Metrics:** Establish clear performance metrics for staff, and regularly assess their performance. Recognize and reward high performers.

- **Feedback:** Provide constructive feedback to employees to help them improve and excel in their roles.

5. **Labor Laws Compliance:**

   - **Fair Labor Standards Act (FLSA):** Ensure compliance with labor laws, including minimum wage, overtime pay, and break requirements.

   - **Employee Classification:** Properly classify employees as either exempt or non-exempt, depending on their eligibility for overtime pay.

6. **Employee Engagement:**

   - **Team Building:** Foster a positive work environment through team-building activities and open communication.

   - **Recognition and Rewards:** Recognize and reward employees for their hard work, which can boost morale and motivation.

7. **Technology Integration:**

   - **POS System:** Integrate a point-of-sale system to streamline order processing and improve accuracy in tracking sales and labor costs.

   - **Scheduling Software:** Use scheduling software to optimize staff schedules and manage shifts efficiently.

8. **Labor Cost Control:**

   - **Budgeting:** Set realistic labour budgets based on historical data and business projections.

   - **Monitor and Adjust:** Regularly monitor labour costs against budgets and adjust staffing levels as needed.

9. **Communication:**

   - **Open Communication Channels:** Maintain open lines of communication between management and staff to address concerns and foster a collaborative environment.

   - **Regular Meetings:** Conduct regular staff meetings to discuss performance, address issues, and provide updates.

By effectively managing labour, a restaurant can optimize its operations, provide better service, and enhance overall profitability. Regularly review and adjust your labour management strategies based on changing business conditions and customer demands.

Recruiting Restaurant Staff

Recruiting restaurant staff is a crucial process that requires careful planning and consideration. Here's a step-by-step guide to help you with the recruitment process for restaurant staff:

1. **Define Positions and Roles:**

   - Clearly outline the positions you need to fill, such as servers, chefs, kitchen staff, bartenders, hosts, and managers.

   - Clearly define the roles and responsibilities associated with each position.

2. **Create Job Descriptions:**

   - Write detailed job descriptions for each position, including key responsibilities, qualifications, and any specific skills required.

   - Highlight any unique aspects of your restaurant that might attract potential candidates.

3. **Utilize Multiple Channels for Job Posting:**

   - Post your job openings on popular job boards, your restaurant's website, and social media platforms.

   - Consider local community boards, culinary schools, and industry-specific websites.

4. **Networking:**

   - Leverage your professional network and connections in the industry to find potential candidates.

   - Attend industry events, job fairs, and culinary schools to meet potential candidates.

5. **Screen Resumes and Applications:**

- Review resumes and applications to shortlist candidates who meet the basic requirements.

- Look for relevant experience, skills, and a genuine interest in the restaurant industry.

6. **Conduct Initial Interviews:**

- Conduct phone or initial video interviews to assess candidates' communication skills, enthusiasm, and cultural fit.

- Ask questions related to their experience, availability, and reasons for wanting to work at your restaurant.

7. **Skills Assessment:**

- Depending on the position, consider practical skills assessments or trials to evaluate candidates' abilities.

- For example, you might ask chefs to prepare a sample dish or servers to demonstrate their customer service skills.

8. **In-Person Interviews:**

- Conduct in-person interviews with the shortlisted candidates to further assess their personality, work ethic, and interpersonal skills.

- Include key team members in the interview process to ensure a good fit with the existing staff.

9. **Check References:**

- Contact the references provided by the candidates to verify their work history, reliability, and performance.

10. **Training and Orientation:**

- Once you've selected candidates, provide thorough training and orientation to familiarize them with your restaurant's policies, procedures, and culture.

11. **Continuous Communication:**

- Maintain open communication with your new hires during their initial days to address any concerns or questions.

12. Trial Period:

- Consider implementing a trial period for new hires to ensure they can adapt to the restaurant's environment and meet performance expectations.

Remember, creating a positive and inclusive workplace culture is key to attracting and retaining top talent in the restaurant industry. Regularly assess your recruitment and onboarding processes to make improvements based on feedback and evolving industry standards.

The organizational structure

The organizational structure of a restaurant can vary depending on its size, type, and management style. However, I can provide a general overview of the common roles and departments found in a typical restaurant organization structure:

1. **Owner/Proprietor/Investors:**

   - Responsible for overall business strategy, financial decisions, and long-term planning.

2. **Board of Directors/Advisory Board:**

   - Provides guidance and strategic advice to the owner or management.

3. **General Manager:**

   - Oversees the day-to-day operations of the restaurant.

   - Manages and coordinates staff.

   - Ensures adherence to budgets and financial goals.

   - Handles customer service issues.

4. **Front-of-House (FOH) Staff:**

   - Restaurant Manager:

     Responsible for the front-of-house operations.

     Manages host/hostess, servers, and bartenders.

   - Host/Hostess:

     Greets and seats customers.

     Manages reservations.

   - Servers/Waitstaff:

     Takes orders and serves food.

Provides customer service.

- Bartenders:

    Prepares and serves drinks at the bar.

    Handles cash transactions.

5. **Back-of-House (BOH) Staff:**

- Chef/Head Chef:

    Manages kitchen operations.

    Designs menus and oversees food preparation.

- Sous Chef:

    Assists the head chef.

    Manages kitchen staff.

- Line Cooks:

    Prepares and cooks specific types of food.

- Dishwashers:

    Cleans and maintains kitchen equipment.

    Washes dishes and utensils.

6. **Support Staff:**

- Cleaners/Janitors:

    Maintain cleanliness in the dining and kitchen areas.

- Maintenance Staff:

    Handles repairs and maintenance of the facility.

- Security:

    Ensures the safety and security of the restaurant.

7. **Administrative Staff:**

- Accountant/Bookkeeper:

    Manages financial transactions and records.

- Human Resources (HR):

    Handles employee hiring, training, and payroll.

- Office Manager:

    Manages administrative tasks.

8. **Marketing and Sales:**

   - Marketing Manager:

       Develops marketing strategies.

       Manages promotions and advertising.

   - Sales Team:

       Promotes the restaurant and its services.

9. **IT/Technology Staff:**

   - Manages the restaurant's technology infrastructure, including POS systems and online platforms.

10. **Quality Control/Inspection:**

    - Monitors food quality and ensures adherence to health and safety standards.

This structure can vary based on the size and complexity of the restaurant. Smaller establishments may have fewer specialized roles, and some positions may be combined, while larger establishments may have more layers of management and specialized departments.

The Job Description of a Head Chef

The job description of a head chef, also known as an executive chef, typically includes a wide range of responsibilities related to the overall management and operation of a kitchen. The specific duties may vary depending on the size and type of the establishment, such as a restaurant, hotel, catering service, or other food service facilities. Here is a comprehensive overview of the key aspects of a head chef's job description:

1. **Culinary Leadership:**

   - Develop and plan menus, taking into consideration factors like seasonality, cost, and customer preferences.

   - Oversee the preparation and presentation of dishes to ensure high-quality standards.

   - Provide creative input for new recipes and dishes.

2. **Kitchen Management:**

   - Manage and coordinate all kitchen activities, including food preparation, cooking, and sanitation.

   - Supervise kitchen staff, including chefs, cooks, and kitchen assistants, and provide training as needed.

   - Create and maintain a positive and efficient work environment.

3. **Quality Control:**

   - Ensure that all dishes meet the established quality standards and specifications.

   - Implement and enforce food safety and hygiene regulations to maintain a clean and safe kitchen.

4. **Inventory and Cost Management:**

   - Control and manage inventory levels to minimize waste and optimize costs.

- Monitor food costs and work towards achieving budgetary goals.

5. **Supplier Relations:**

- Establish and maintain relationships with food suppliers to ensure the availability of high-quality ingredients.

- Negotiate contracts and pricing with vendors.

6. **Menu Planning and Development:**

- Create and update menus based on market trends, customer feedback, and seasonal availability.

- Introduce new dishes and culinary concepts to keep the menu fresh and appealing.

7. **Staff Development:**

- Recruit, train, and develop kitchen staff.

- Conduct performance evaluations and provide constructive feedback.

- Foster a collaborative and positive team culture.

8. **Administrative Tasks:**

- Handle administrative tasks such as scheduling, payroll, and budget management.

- Ensure compliance with all relevant regulations, including health and safety standards.

9. **Customer Relations:**

- Interact with customers to gather feedback and address any concerns or special requests.

- Collaborate with front-of-house staff to enhance the overall dining experience.

10. **Adaptability:**

- Stay informed about industry trends and incorporate innovative culinary techniques and concepts.

Overall, a head chef plays a crucial role in the success of a culinary establishment by combining culinary expertise with effective leadership and management skills.

Appendix G
Key Qualities of Restaurateur

Running a successful restaurant requires a combination of various skills and qualities. Here are some key qualities that a restaurateur should possess:

1. **Passion for Food and Hospitality:**

   - A genuine love for food and a passion for creating a positive dining experience for customers.

2. **Business Acumen:**

   - Strong business sense and financial acumen to manage the financial aspects of the restaurant, such as budgeting, pricing, and cost control.

3. **Customer Focus:**

   - A customer-centric mindset, focusing on providing excellent customer service and ensuring customer satisfaction.

4. **Leadership Skills:**

   - The ability to lead and manage a team effectively, including chefs, kitchen staff, servers, and other employees.

5. **Communication Skills:**

   - Effective communication with both customers and staff is crucial. Clear communication helps in creating a positive work environment and delivering a consistent message to customers.

6. **Adaptability:**

   - The restaurant industry can be dynamic and subject to changes. A successful restaurateur should be adaptable to new trends, customer preferences, and industry changes.

7. **Creativity:**

- Innovation in menu design, marketing strategies, and overall restaurant concept can set a restaurant apart from competitors.

8. **Attention to Detail:**

- Success often lies in the details. Being meticulous about the quality of ingredients, presentation, and service is essential.

9. **Problem-Solving Skills:**

- Quick and effective problem-solving skills are crucial in handling unexpected issues that may arise in a restaurant operation.

10. **Networking Skills:**

- Building and maintaining relationships with suppliers, local businesses, and the community can be beneficial for a restaurant's success.

11. **Time Management:**

- Efficient time management is essential for handling various aspects of the restaurant, from daily operations to long-term planning.

12. **Understanding of Regulations:**

- Knowledge of health and safety regulations, food safety standards, and compliance with local laws is necessary to run a legal and safe establishment.

13. **Marketing and Promotion:**

- The ability to effectively market the restaurant and create promotional strategies to attract and retain customers.

14. **Resilience:**

- The restaurant industry can be challenging, with its ups and downs. Resilience and the ability to handle stress and setbacks are important.

15. **Continuous Learning:**

- Keeping up with industry trends, staying informed about new cooking techniques, and being open to learning and evolving.

Remember that successful restaurants often embody a combination of these qualities, and ongoing commitment to improvement and customer satisfaction is key to long-term success.

Appendix H
Top 50 Challenges in the Restaurant Business

Running a restaurant comes with a multitude of challenges, and the specific difficulties can vary based on location, concept, and scale. Here's a list of 50 challenges that are commonly faced by those in the restaurant business:

1. **Competition:** Fierce competition in the restaurant industry can make it challenging to stand out.

2. **Changing Consumer Preferences:** Adapting to evolving tastes and preferences of customers.

3. **Economic Downturns:** Restaurants are often vulnerable to economic fluctuations.

4. **Staffing Issues:** Recruiting, training, and retaining skilled and reliable staff.

5. **High Turnover Rates:** Frequent turnover of staff can lead to consistency and training challenges.

6. **Rising Costs:** Fluctuating food and labour costs impact profitability.

7. **Supply Chain Disruptions:** Issues with obtaining consistent and quality ingredients.

8. **Health and Safety Compliance:** Strict adherence to health and safety regulations.

9. **Technology Integration:** Keeping up with technology trends for online orders, reservations, and management systems.

10. **Marketing and Branding:** Creating and maintaining a strong brand image to attract customers.

11. **Customer Reviews:** Managing online reviews and addressing negative feedback.

12. **Menu Development:** Offering diverse and appealing menu items that cater to different preferences.

13. **Quality Control:** Ensuring consistent food quality and service.

14. **Sustainability:** Meeting growing demands for environmentally friendly practices.

15. **Licensing and Permits:** Navigating the legal requirements for operation.

16. **Crisis Management:** Dealing with unexpected situations such as accidents or natural disasters.

17. **Waste Management:** Reducing food and material waste.

18. **Technology Security:** Protecting customer data and online transactions.

19. **Community Engagement:** Building and maintaining positive relationships with the local community.

20. **Trends and Innovation:** Staying ahead of industry trends to remain relevant.

21. **Dietary Restrictions:** Catering to various dietary needs and restrictions.

22. **Delivery Challenges:** Managing food quality and delivery logistics for takeout and delivery services.

23. **Government Regulations:** Navigating complex and ever-changing regulations.

24. **Rising Rent Costs:** Escalating costs of leasing or owning restaurant space.

25. **Location Selection:** Choosing the right location with the right target demographic.

26. **Customer Retention:** Encouraging repeat business and customer loyalty.

27. **Social Media Management:** Effectively using social media for marketing and communication.

28. **Training Programs:** Developing effective training programs for staff.

29. **Cultural Sensitivity:** Being aware of and respecting diverse cultural nuances.

30. **Seasonal Fluctuations:** Adapting to variations in customer traffic during different seasons.

31. **Financial Management:** Ensuring sound financial practices and budgeting.

32. **Labor Laws:** Compliance with labor laws and regulations.

33. **Insurance Costs:** Managing insurance costs for property, liability, and employee coverage.

34. **Technology Maintenance:** Regular maintenance and updates for restaurant technology.

35. **Tax Compliance:** Staying informed about and compliant with tax regulations.

36. **Payment Processing:** Efficient and secure payment processing systems.

37. **Fraud Prevention:** Protecting against fraudulent activities.

38. **Employee Morale:** Maintaining a positive work environment and employee satisfaction.

39. **Local Partnerships:** Collaborating with local businesses for mutual benefits.

40. **Lack of Innovation:** Failing to adapt to changing customer expectations.

41. **Crisis Communication:** Handling public relations during crises.

42. **Food Safety:** Ensuring safe food handling practices.

43. **Accessibility:** Addressing the needs of customers with disabilities.

44. **Cultural Trends:** Staying informed about cultural trends that may impact the business.

45. **Space Utilization:** Efficiently using available space for maximum capacity.

46. **Volatile Food Prices:** Fluctuations in the cost of key ingredients.

47. **Alcohol Licensing:** Managing the complexities of serving alcoholic beverages.

48. **Work-Life Balance:** Balancing the demands of running a restaurant with personal life.

49. **Data Security:** Protecting customer and business data from breaches.

50. **Evolving Consumer Behaviour:** Adapting to changes in how customers prefer to dine and order.

Success in the restaurant industry often involves navigating these challenges with creativity, resilience, and a customer-centric approach.

Top 25 Effective Marketing, Advertising, and Visibility Strategies for a Successful Restaurant

Creating a successful marketing and advertising strategy for a restaurant involves a combination of traditional and digital approaches. Here are 25 effective marketing, advertising, and visibility strategies for a restaurant:

1. **Unique Selling Proposition (USP):** Clearly define what makes your restaurant stand out, and highlight it in all your marketing materials.

2. **Online Presence:**

   - Develop a professional website with a user-friendly interface.

   - Optimize the website for search engines (SEO) to improve visibility.

3. **Social Media Marketing:**

   - Leverage popular platforms like Facebook, Instagram, Twitter, and TikTok.

   - Share high-quality photos, videos, and engage with your audience.

4. **Google My Business:**

   - Claim and optimize your Google My Business listing to appear in local searches.

   - Encourage customers to leave positive reviews.

5. **Local Partnerships:**

   - Collaborate with local businesses and organizations for cross-promotions.

   - Sponsor local events to increase visibility.

6. **Email Marketing:**

- Build and maintain an email list to send updates, promotions, and special offers.

- Implement personalized email campaigns.

7. **Loyalty Programs:**

- Create a loyalty program to encourage repeat customers.

- Offer discounts or free items after a certain number of visits.

8. **Influencer Marketing:**

- Partner with local influencers or food bloggers to review and promote your restaurant.

- Encourage user-generated content by offering incentives.

9. **Geo-Targeted Ads:**

- Use location-based advertising to target potential customers in your area.

- Run ads on platforms like Facebook, Instagram, and Google Ads.

10. **Content Marketing:**

- Start a blog on your website with engaging content related to your cuisine or industry.

- Share recipes, behind-the-scenes stories, and cooking tips.

11. **Visual Branding:**

- Invest in professional and consistent branding across all platforms.

- Use eye-catching visuals in menus, posters, and online content.

12. **Events and Promotions:**

- Host special events, theme nights, or promotions to attract new customers.

- Advertise these events through social media and local channels.

13. Mobile-Friendly Strategy:

- Ensure your website and online ordering system are mobile-friendly.

- Consider creating a dedicated mobile app for easier ordering.

14. Customer Testimonials:

- Showcase positive reviews and testimonials in your marketing materials.

- Encourage satisfied customers to leave reviews on platforms like Yelp and TripAdvisor.

15. Strategic Signage:

- Utilize outdoor and indoor signage to attract foot traffic.

- Include QR codes for easy access to your online menu or promotions.

16. Collaborative Marketing:

- Partner with delivery services or food apps for increased visibility.

- Offer exclusive deals through these platforms.

17. Community Engagement:

- Participate in local community events and sponsorships.

- Donate to local charities and involve your restaurant in community initiatives.

18. Google Ads Campaigns:

- Run targeted Google Ads campaigns based on relevant keywords.

- Utilize Google Ad Extensions for additional information.

19. Employee Advocacy:

- Encourage your staff to share positive experiences on social media.

- Highlight team members and their contributions.

20. **Online Reservations:**

- Use online reservation platforms to make it easy for customers to book a table.

- Offer special promotions for online reservations.

21. **Seasonal Specials:**

- Introduce seasonal menu items and promotions to keep things fresh.

- Advertise these specials through social media and in-restaurant signage.

22. **Interactive Menus:**

- Use QR codes on menus to provide access to online reviews, chef profiles, or videos.

- Implement augmented reality (AR) features for an interactive dining experience.

23. **Feedback and Improvement:**

- Collect customer feedback and use it to make improvements.

- Showcase how you've responded to feedback to build trust.

24. **Catering Services:**

- Promote your restaurant's catering services for events, parties, and business meetings.

- Create catering-specific marketing materials.

25. **Data Analytics:**

- Use analytics tools to track the performance of your marketing campaigns.

- Adjust strategies based on data insights for continuous improvement

Appendix J
Target Customers

The target Customers of a restaurant is typically defined by factors such as the type of cuisine offered, the atmosphere, location, pricing, and overall concept. Here are some common categories of target audiences for different types of restaurants:

1. **Fine Dining Restaurant:**

    - **Demographic:** Affluent individuals, professionals, and couples celebrating special occasions.

    - **Psychographic:** People who appreciate gourmet cuisine, exquisite ambiance, and personalized service.

    - **Geographic:** Located in upscale neighbourhoods or city centres.

2. **Casual Dining Restaurant:**

    - **Demographic:** Families, working professionals, and groups of friends.

    - **Psychographic:** Individuals seeking a relaxed and informal dining experience without the formality of fine dining.

    - **Geographic:** Positioned in both suburban and urban areas.

3. **Fast Casual Restaurant:**

    - **Demographic:** Busy professionals, students, and individuals looking for quick, healthier alternatives.

    - **Psychographic:** People who value speed, convenience, and quality in their dining experience.

    - **Geographic:** Often located in commercial areas, near offices, or college campuses.

4. **Ethnic or Specialty Restaurant:**

   - **Demographic:** Individuals interested in a specific cuisine or cultural experience.

   - **Psychographic:** People who enjoy exploring diverse Flavors and cultural nuances in food.

   - **Geographic:** May be situated in neighbourhoods with a diverse population or in areas where there's interest in the specific cuisine.

5. **Family-Friendly Restaurant:**

   - **Demographic:** Families with children, young parents, and groups with kids.

   - **Psychographic:** Individuals looking for a welcoming environment and menu options suitable for all ages.

   - **Geographic:** Positioned in family-friendly neighbourhoods or near family-oriented attractions.

6. **Gourmet or Niche Restaurant:**

   - **Demographic:** Food enthusiasts, culinary adventurers, and those seeking unique dining experiences.

   - **Psychographic:** Individuals who appreciate rare ingredients, artistic presentation, and innovative culinary techniques.

   - **Geographic:** Typically found in urban areas with a discerning food culture.

Understanding the target audience is crucial for marketing strategies, menu development, and overall branding. Restaurants often tailor their offerings, ambiance, and promotional activities to attract and retain their intended customer base.

Appendix K
Communication

Differentiating communication for a restaurant involves highlighting unique aspects that set it apart from competitors and creating a compelling message that resonates with the target audience. Here are some strategies:

1. **Culinary Identity:**

   - Emphasize the unique Flavors, ingredients, or cooking techniques that define the restaurant's cuisine.

   - Highlight any special dishes or signature creations that customers can only experience at your restaurant.

2. **Ambiance and Atmosphere:**

   - Showcase the restaurant's interior design, ambiance, or theme that creates a distinctive dining experience.

   - Use visuals, such as high-quality photos or videos, to give potential customers a glimpse of the atmosphere.

3. **Customer Experience:**

   - Emphasize exceptional customer service and personalized experiences.

   - Share positive customer reviews or testimonials that highlight the unique aspects of their dining experience.

4. **Local Sourcing and Sustainability:**

   - Communicate a commitment to using locally sourced, organic, or sustainable ingredients.

   - Share stories about partnerships with local farmers or initiatives that support environmental sustainability.

5. **Culinary Events and Experiences:**

   - Promote special events, themed nights, or chef's table experiences that set your restaurant apart.

   - Highlight any cooking classes, tastings, or collaborations with renowned chefs.

6. **Technology Integration:**

   - If applicable, showcase any innovative technology used in the kitchen or for customer interactions, such as online ordering, a mobile app, or digital menu options.

7. **Cultural Engagement:**

   - Connect with the local community by participating in or sponsoring cultural events, festivals, or charity initiatives.

   - Highlight any cultural influences in the cuisine or décor.

8. **Social Media Presence:**

   - Maintain an active presence on social media platforms to engage with the audience.

   - Share behind-the-scenes glimpses, chef stories, and customer stories to humanize the brand.

9. **Exclusive Offers and Loyalty Programs:**

   - Create exclusive offers or loyalty programs to reward repeat customers.

   - Emphasize any special discounts, promotions, or unique loyalty perks.

10. **Storytelling:**

   - Craft a compelling narrative that tells the story of the restaurant, its founders, or the inspiration behind the menu.

   - Use storytelling in marketing materials, on the website, and in social media posts.

Remember, consistency is key. Ensure that the differentiating factors are communicated across all touchpoints, from the website and social media to the physical restaurant space.

Appendix L

Eliminating or Minimising the Waste = Profit

Minimizing waste in a restaurant is not only environmentally responsible but can also significantly contribute to increased profits. Here are some strategies to help reduce waste in your restaurant:

1. **Inventory Management:**

   - Implement a robust inventory management system to track and control the usage of ingredients. This helps prevent overordering and spoilage.

2. **Menu Planning:**

   - Design your menu with an emphasis on using seasonal and local ingredients. This reduces the likelihood of excess inventory and waste.

3. **Portion Control:**

   - Train staff to use consistent portion sizes to avoid both over-serving and customer dissatisfaction. This helps manage food costs and reduces plate waste.

4. **Creative Use of Leftovers:**

   - Develop creative ways to use leftovers or surplus ingredients in daily specials or new menu items. This can turn what might have been waste into profitable dishes.

5. **Collaborate with Local Farms or Food Banks:**

   - Establish relationships with local farms to repurpose food scraps for compost or animal feed. Alternatively, consider donating excess food to food banks or shelters.

6. **Employee Training:**

   - Train your staff to be mindful of waste and encourage them to suggest ways to reduce it. Ensure they are educated on proper storage and handling procedures to extend the shelf life of ingredients.

7. **Technology Solutions:**

   - Use technology to monitor and analyze purchasing and consumption patterns. This can help identify areas where waste can be minimized.

8. **Recycling and Composting:**

   - Implement a comprehensive recycling and composting program. This not only reduces landfill waste but can also save on waste disposal costs.

9. **Energy Efficiency:**

   - Optimize kitchen equipment for energy efficiency to reduce utility costs. Upgrading to energy-efficient appliances can result in long-term savings.

10. **Customer Education:**

    - Inform customers about your commitment to reducing waste and encourage them to support your efforts. This can create a positive image for your restaurant and attract environmentally conscious patrons.

11. **Regular Audits:**

    - Conduct regular waste audits to identify patterns and areas for improvement. This ongoing assessment helps in fine-tuning your waste reduction strategies.

Remember that a successful waste reduction strategy involves a combination of careful planning, staff training, and ongoing evaluation of practices. By making waste reduction a priority, your restaurant can not only contribute to a more sustainable environment but also improve its overall profitability. It is the main profit creating source

Appendix M

Collaborating with Food Aggregators

Collaborating with food aggregators can be a strategic move for various businesses in the food industry. Food aggregators are platforms that connect customers with a variety of restaurants and food providers, allowing users to browse menus, place orders, and often arrange for food delivery. Here are some aspects to consider when exploring collaborations with food aggregators:

1. **Increased Visibility:**

   - Partnering with popular food aggregators can significantly increase your visibility among potential customers. These platforms often have a large user base actively seeking dining options.

2. **Online Ordering and Delivery:**

   - Food aggregators usually provide online ordering and delivery services, which can be beneficial if your business doesn't have its own delivery infrastructure. This can save you the hassle and cost of managing your own delivery fleet.

3. **Marketing and Promotion:**

   - Aggregators often engage in marketing and promotional activities to attract users. Collaborating with them may give your business exposure through these marketing efforts, helping you reach a broader audience.

4. **Customer Reviews and Ratings:**

   - Customer reviews and ratings on food aggregator platforms can influence potential customers. Ensure your products and services are of high quality to maintain positive reviews and ratings.

5. **Technology Integration:**

   - Integrate your systems with the aggregator's platform to streamline the order process. This may involve using APIs

(Application Programming Interfaces) to connect your ordering and inventory systems with the aggregator's platform.

6. **Data Analytics:**

   - Leverage data analytics provided by the aggregator to gain insights into customer behavior, preferences, and order patterns. This information can help you refine your offerings and marketing strategies.

7. **Negotiate Terms:**

   - When collaborating with food aggregators, carefully review and negotiate terms such as commission rates, delivery charges, and any other fees associated with the partnership. Understand the financial implications for your business.

8. **Maintain Brand Consistency:**

   - While collaborating with food aggregators, ensure that your brand identity, product quality, and customer service standards remain consistent. Consistency across platforms is crucial for building trust and loyalty.

9. **Legal and Regulatory Compliance:**

   - Stay informed about local laws and regulations governing food delivery and online platforms. Ensure that your collaboration complies with these regulations.

10. **Evaluate Performance:**

    - Regularly assess the performance of your collaboration with food aggregators. Track key performance indicators (KPIs) such as order volume, customer satisfaction, and return on investment to gauge the success of the partnership.

Remember that collaboration with food aggregators is just one strategy, and its effectiveness depends on your business model, target audience, and market conditions. It's essential to continually evaluate and adjust your approach based on results and changing circumstances.

Check Points

Starting a restaurant involves careful planning and execution. Here's a breakdown of key checkpoints for the restaurant business, covering the period prior to opening, during the opening, and post-opening:

Prior to Opening:

1. **Market Research and Concept Development:**
   - Conduct thorough market research to understand the target audience, competition, and trends.
   - Develop a unique concept that sets your restaurant apart.

2. **Business Plan:**
   - Create a comprehensive business plan outlining your concept, target market, financial projections, and marketing strategy.

3. **Location Selection:**
   - Choose a strategic location based on the target market, foot traffic, and accessibility.

4. **Legal Requirements:**
   - Obtain all necessary licenses and permits, including health permits, alcohol licenses, and business permits.

5. **Menu Development:**
   - Create a menu that aligns with your concept and appeals to your target audience.

6. **Supplier Partnerships:**
   - Establish relationships with reliable suppliers for food, beverages, and other essential items.

7. **Interior Design and Layout:**

- Design an appealing and functional interior layout that complements your concept.

8. **Hiring and Training:**

   - Recruit and train staff, ensuring they understand the concept, menu, and service standards.

During the Opening:

1. **Soft Opening:**

   - Conduct a soft opening to identify and address any operational issues before the grand opening.

2. **Marketing and Promotion:**

   - Execute a robust marketing plan to create awareness, attract customers, and generate buzz.

3. **Quality Control:**

   - Monitor food and service quality closely during the initial days and make necessary adjustments.

4. **Customer Feedback:**

   - Collect feedback from customers to identify areas for improvement.

5. **Staff Oversight:**

   - Ensure that staff members are performing well and address any issues promptly.

6. **Inventory Management:**

   - Implement effective inventory management to control costs and reduce waste.

Post Opening:

1. **Financial Evaluation:**

   - Analyze financial performance against projections and adjust budgets accordingly.

2. **Customer Loyalty Programs:**

   - Implement loyalty programs to retain customers and encourage repeat business.

3. **Continuous Improvement:**

   - Regularly review operations and make improvements based on customer feedback and industry trends.

4. **Community Engagement:**

   - Engage with the local community through events, sponsorships, and collaborations.

5. **Adapt to Market Changes:**

   - Stay informed about market trends and be ready to adapt the menu or concept accordingly.

6. **Technology Integration:**

   - Embrace technology for efficient operations, online ordering, and reservations.

7. **Staff Development:**

   - Invest in ongoing training and development for staff to maintain high standards.

Remember, the restaurant industry is dynamic, and staying adaptable is key to long-term success. Regularly reassess your business strategies and make adjustments as needed.

Appendix O
Consideration Factors

The restaurant business is multifaceted and involves various factors that contribute to its success or failure. Here are numerous factors to consider:

1. **Location:**
   - Accessibility and visibility
   - Demographics of the area
   - Proximity to competitors

2. **Concept and Cuisine:**
   - The type of cuisine offered
   - Unique selling proposition (USP)
   - Target market and customer preferences

3. **Menu Design:**
   - Variety and pricing
   - Seasonal adjustments
   - Dietary considerations (e.g., vegetarian, gluten-free options)

4. **Quality of Food:**
   - Consistency in taste and presentation
   - Sourcing of ingredients
   - Food safety and hygiene

5. **Service:**
   - Efficient and friendly staff
   - Training programs for employees
   - Speed of service and order accuracy

6. **Ambiance and Atmosphere:**
   - Interior design and decor
   - Lighting and music
   - Comfort and cleanliness

7. **Marketing and Branding:**
   - Online presence (website, social media)
   - Advertising and promotions
   - Brand image and reputation management

8. **Technology:**
   - Point-of-sale (POS) systems
   - Online ordering and delivery platforms
   - Reservation systems

9. **Licensing and Compliance:**
   - Adherence to health codes
   - Alcohol licensing (if applicable)
   - Employment regulations

10. **Cost Management:**
    - Controlling food and labour costs
    - Negotiating with suppliers
    - Energy and utility management

11. **Financial Management:**
    - Budgeting and forecasting
    - Cash flow management
    - Pricing strategy

12. **Customer Feedback and Reviews:**
    - Gathering and analyzing customer feedback
    - Addressing negative reviews promptly
    - Implementing improvements based on feedback

13. **Employee Satisfaction and Retention:**

- Creating a positive work environment
- Training and development opportunities
- Competitive wages and benefits

14. **Community Engagement:**

- Involvement in local events
- Sponsorships and partnerships
- Building relationships with neighbouring businesses

15. **Adaptability and Innovation:**

- Keeping up with industry trends
- Updating menu and services
- Embracing new technologies

16. **Economic Factors:**

- Monitoring economic trends
- Adapting to inflation and changes in consumer spending

17. **Sustainability Practices:**

- Environmentally friendly practices
- Ethical sourcing of ingredients
- Waste reduction and recycling initiatives

Considering and effectively managing these factors can contribute to the long-term success of a restaurant business. It's important for restaurant owners and managers to continually assess and adapt to changes in the market and consumer preferences.

Appendix
Monthly Financial Components Tracking sheet

Note: For reference only & customize as per your needs

1 Food Costs

Ingredients

Food Preparation

2   Labor Costs

Chefs & cooks

Servers

Cleaners & Temporary staff

3   Overhead Costs

Rent and Utilities (Gas/water/Elec/Air)

Insurances

Key person Insurance

Licenses and Permits

4   Equipment Costs

Purchase

Maintenance

Transportation

5   Marketing and Advertising

Promotion

11   **Contingency and Miscellaneous**

        Unexpected Expenses

12   **Health & safety**

        Accidental or injuries hospital exp

        Safety PPE (Personal protective equipment)

13   **Welfare & Bonus**

        Uniforms

        Awards & Recognitions

        Employee Birthday

        Yearly Bonus

        Increments (Performance Appraisal)

        indoor Boardgames

        Accommodation

14   **Audits & consultants**

        3 rd. party Audit

        Consultation reports

15   **Finance**

        WACC

        Forex conversion

        Bank Related

16   **IT Related**

        Cloud

        ERP

Cyber security

AI implementation

Internet Unlimited

Mobile phones

Recharges

Subscriptions

17 **External**

Local Donations for community

School children support

Religious houses

18 **Imports**

Custom handling charges

Import Duty

19 **Legal**

fee

Advisory

Fines

Penalties

20 **Taxes**

Direct

Indirect (GST/VAT/Cess)

21 **Net Profit**

Appendix Q
Green Restaurant

A "Green Restaurant" is a dining establishment committed to sustainability and environmental responsibility. These restaurants strive to minimize their ecological footprint by integrating eco-friendly practices throughout their operations. The goal is not only to provide high-quality, delicious food but also to contribute positively to the environment and promote a sustainable future.

Key Practices of a Green Restaurant

1. **Sustainable Sourcing**

   - **Local and Organic Ingredients**: Sourcing ingredients from local farms and producers reduces transportation emissions and supports the local economy. Organic ingredients are grown without harmful pesticides, promoting healthier ecosystems.

   - **Seasonal Menus**: Designing menus around seasonal produce reduces the need for energy-intensive storage and transportation, ensuring fresher and more nutritious meals.

2. **Waste Reduction**

   - **Composting**: Food scraps and organic waste are composted, turning waste into valuable soil instead of sending it to landfills.

   - **Recycling**: Restaurants implement comprehensive recycling programs for glass, paper, plastics, and other materials to reduce landfill waste.

   - **Minimizing Single-Use Items**: Reducing or eliminating single-use plastics and other disposable items helps decrease environmental pollution. Alternatives like biodegradable or reusable containers are used.

3. **Energy Efficiency**

- **Efficient Appliances**: Using energy-efficient kitchen equipment, lighting, and HVAC systems lowers energy consumption and reduces the restaurant's carbon footprint.

- **Renewable Energy**: Some green restaurants invest in renewable energy sources like solar or wind power to meet their energy needs.

4. **Water Conservation**

- **Low-Flow Fixtures**: Installing low-flow faucets and toilets reduces water usage.

- **Greywater Reuse**: Implementing systems that reuse greywater (water from sinks, dishwashers, etc.) for non-potable purposes, such as irrigation.

5. **Eco-Friendly Materials**

- **Sustainable Building Materials**: Using recycled, reclaimed, or sustainably sourced materials in the construction and furnishing of the restaurant.

- **Green Cleaning Products**: Utilizing non-toxic, biodegradable cleaning products to maintain a healthy indoor environment and reduce pollution.

6. **Community Engagement and Education**

- **Customer Education**: Informing customers about the restaurant's sustainability practices and encouraging eco-friendly behaviors.

- **Community Involvement**: Engaging with the local community through partnerships, education, and events that promote sustainability.

7. **Ethical Practices**

- **Fair Trade and Humane Treatment**: Sourcing products that are Fair Trade certified and ensuring that meat and dairy products come from animals that are humanely treated.

Benefits of Green Restaurant Practices

- **Environmental Impact**: Significantly reduces the restaurant's carbon footprint, conserves resources, and minimizes waste.

- **Healthier Options**: Provides customers with healthier, fresher, and more nutritious meals.

- **Cost Savings**: Long-term cost savings through reduced energy and water consumption, and waste disposal.

- **Brand Loyalty**: Attracts eco-conscious customers and builds a positive brand reputation.

Green restaurants not only contribute to environmental sustainability but also create a healthier, more ethical dining experience for their customers.

Appendix R
Sustainable Development Goals (SDGs)

The restaurant industry can contribute to several Sustainable Development Goals (SDGs) outlined by the United Nations. Here's how the industry aligns with specific SDGs:

1. SDG 2: Zero Hunger

Contribution: Restaurants can help by sourcing food locally and reducing food waste, thus ensuring a more sustainable food supply chain. They can also offer nutritious and affordable food options to the community.

2. SDG 3: Good Health and Well-being

Contribution: By promoting healthy eating habits and offering balanced, nutritious meals, restaurants can play a role in improving public health.

3. SDG 8: Decent Work and Economic Growth

Contribution: The restaurant industry is a major employer worldwide. Ensuring fair wages, safe working conditions, and opportunities for career growth supports this goal.

4. SDG 12: Responsible Consumption and Production

Contribution: Restaurants can reduce their environmental footprint by minimizing food waste, using sustainable packaging, and sourcing ingredients that are ethically produced.

5. SDG 13: Climate Action

Contribution: Implementing energy-efficient practices, reducing greenhouse gas emissions, and using sustainable food sources can help restaurants contribute to climate action.

6. SDG 14: Life Below Water

Contribution: Restaurants can support sustainable fishing practices and avoid ingredients that contribute to overfishing or harm marine ecosystems.

7. SDG 15: Life on Land

Contribution: Sourcing ingredients from sustainable agriculture and avoiding products linked to deforestation can help preserve terrestrial ecosystems.

8. SDG 17: Partnerships for the Goals

Contribution: Restaurants can collaborate with local communities, NGOs, and governments to promote sustainability initiatives and contribute to the overall achievement of the SDGs.

Incorporating these goals into restaurant operations not only supports global sustainability efforts but can also enhance the brand's reputation and appeal to conscious consumers.

Appendix S
Quotes on the Restaurant Industry Related

1. "In a restaurant, choose a table near a waiter." Jewish Proverb

2. "Going to a restaurant is one of my keenest pleasures. Meeting someplace with old and new friends, ordering wine, eating food, surrounded by strangers, I think is the core of what it means to live a civilized life." – Adam Gopnik, Writer.

3. "There is no love sincerer than the love of food." – George Bernard Shaw, Author.

4. "Fame itself… doesn't really afford you anything more than a good seat in a restaurant." – David Bowie, Singer.

5. "When you go to a restaurant, the less you know about what happens in the kitchen, the more you enjoy your meal." – Jeffrey Wright, Actor.

6. "If you want a reliable tip, drive into a town, go to the nearest appliance store, and seek out the dishwasher repair man. He spends a lot of time in restaurant kitchens and usually has strong opinions about them." – Bryan Miller, Television Writer.

7. "Food is our common ground, a universal experience." -James Beard, Chef and Author.

8. "Sharing food with another human being is an intimate act that should not be indulged in lightly." -M. F. K. Fisher, Food Writer.

9. "The only thing I like better than talking about food is eating." – John Walters, Broadcaster.

10. "After a good dinner one can forgive anybody, even one's own relations." – Oscar Wilde, Author.

11. "I want to enjoy my life, and food is a big part of it." – Gwyneth Paltrow, Actress.

12. "My weaknesses have always been food and men – in that order." – Dolly Parton, Singer and Philanthropist.

13. "People who love to eat are always the best people." – Julia Child, Chef, Author, and Television Host.

14. "Every restaurant is a theatre, and the truly great ones allow us to indulge in the fantasy that we are rich and powerful. When restaurants hold up their end of the bargain, they give us the illusion of being surrounded by servants' intent on ensuring our happiness and offering extraordinary food. But even modest restaurants offer the opportunity to become someone else, at least for a little while. Restaurants free us from mundane reality; that is part of their charm. When you walk through the door, you are entering neutral territory where you are free to be whoever you choose for the duration of the meal." – Ruth Reichl, Restaurant Critic and Author.

15. "Life is like a restaurant; you can have anything you want as long as you are willing to pay the price." – Moffat Machingura, Author.

16. "If I could have dinner with anyone who lived in history, it would depend on the restaurant." – Rodney Dangerfield, Actor and Comedian.

17. "It's easier to be faithful to a restaurant than it is to a woman." – Federico Fellini, Director and Screenwriter.

18. "The trouble with eating Italian is that 5 or 6 days later, you're hungry again." – George Miller, Filmmaker.

19. "There is a difference between dining and eating. Dining is an art. When you eat to get the most out of your meal, to please the palate, just as well as to satiate the appetite, that, my friend, is dining." – Yuan Mei, Painter and Poet.

20. "Stafford's Law of Dining Out states that the second you finish ordering something in a restaurant, food will immediately arrive at an adjacent table that looks ten times better." – Stewart Stafford, Author.

21. "The other night he took me to dinner. We were having a wonderful time when he remarked, "You can certainly tell the wives from the sweethearts." I stopped licking the stream of butter dripping

down my elbow and replied, "What kind of crack is that?" – Erma Bombeck, Author and Humourist.

22. "Good food will always welcome you back with a smile." – Anthony T. Hincks, Author.

23. "Look at your waiter's face. He knows. It's another reason to be polite to your waiter: he could save your life with a raised eyebrow or a sigh." – Anthony Bourdain.

24. "One time, I went to a restaurant and I asked the waiter for some food for thought. He left, came back, and tried shoving a sirloin in my ear." – Travis Jeremiah Dahnke, Writer.

25. "One cannot think well, love well, sleep well, if one has not dined well." – Virginia Woolf, Author.

26. "The discovery of a new dish does more for the happiness of the human race than the discovery of a star." – Jean Anthelme Brillat-Savarin, Philosopher.

27. "It's so beautifully arranged on the plate – you know someone's fingers have been all over it." – Julia Child.

28. "Fools make feasts and wise men eat them." – Benjamin Franklin.

29. "Great restaurants are, of course, nothing but mouth-brothels. There is no point in going to them if one intends to keep one's belt buckled." – Frederic Raphael, Screenwriter.

30. "Although the skills aren't hard to learn, finding the happiness and finding the satisfaction and finding fulfilment in continuously serving somebody else something good to eat, is what makes a really good restaurant." – Mario Batali, Chef.

31. "The business of feeding people is the most amazing business in the world." – José Andrés, Chef and Founder of World Central Kitchen.

32. "There are people with otherwise chaotic and disorganized lives, a certain type of person that's always found a home in the restaurant business in much the same way that a lot of people find a home in the military." – Anthony Bourdain, Chef, Author and Television Show Host.

33. "There's the common misconception that restaurants make a lot of money. It's not true. If you look at maybe the top chef in the world, or at least monetarily, it's like Wolfgang Puck, but he makes as much money as an average crappy investment banker." – David Chang, Chef and Television Host.

34. "Find what's hot, find what's just opened and then look for the worst review of the week. There is so much to learn from watching a restaurant getting absolutely panned and having a bad experience. Go and see it for yourself." – Gordon Ramsey, Chef and Television Host.

35. "You've always got to work to your highest ability level. When times are great and restaurants are jamming, that's when some restaurants get sloppy and take things for granted. Never take things for granted." – Michael Symon, Chef and Television Host.

36. "Let's face it: if you and I have the same capabilities, the same energy, the same staff, if the only thing that's different between you and me is the products we can get, and I can get a better product than you, I'm going to be a better chef." – Thomas Keller, Chef.

37. "Food is one part of the experience. And it has to be somewhere between 50 to 60 percent of the dining experience. But the rest counts as well: The mood, the atmosphere, the music, the feeling, the design, the harmony between what you have on the plate and what surrounds the plate." – Alain Ducasse, Chef.

38. "One of the reasons that people enjoy coming to a great restaurant is that when an extraordinary meal is placed in front of them, they feel honoured, respected, and even a little bit loved." – Marcus Samuelsson, Chef.

39. "One thing I always say is being a great chef today is not enough – you have to be a great businessman." – Wolfgang Puck, Chef.

40. "Customers don't always know what they want. The decline in coffee-drinking was due to the fact that most of the coffee people bought was stale and they weren't enjoying it. Once they tasted ours and experienced what we call "the third place".. a gathering place between home and work where they were treated with respect.. they

found we were filling a need they didn't know they had." – Howard Schultz, CEO of Starbucks.

41. "A restaurant is a fantasy—a kind of living fantasy in which diners are the most important members of the cast." – Warner LeRoy, Businessman.

42. "A good restaurant is like a vacation; it transports you, and it becomes a lot more than just about the food." – Philip Rosenthal, Television Writer and Producer.

43. "If anything is good for pounding humility into you permanently, it's the restaurant business." – Anthony Bourdain.

44. "A restaurant is a fantasy—a kind of living fantasy in which diners are the most important members of the cast." - Warner LeRoy

45. "I judge a restaurant by the bread and by the coffee." - Burt Lancaster

46. "The most essential part of my day is a proper dinner." - Rachael Ray

47. "A restaurant should remove you from the mundane burdens of everyday life and transport you to another world." - Danny Meyer

48. "The only thing I like better than talking about food is eating." - John Walters

49. "Food is not just eating energy. It's an experience." - Guy Fieri

50. "A restaurant is a place where you go to celebrate a special occasion, or to create a new one." - Unknown

51. "Food is our common ground, a universal experience." - James Beard

52. "There is no love sincerer than the love of food." - George Bernard Shaw

53. "There is no better feeling in the world than a warm pizza box on your lap." - Kevin James

54. "Good food is good mood." - Unknown

55. "Eating is a necessity but cooking is an art." - Unknown

56. "A bad day can be made better with some good food." - Unknown

57. "Food is the ingredient that binds us together." - Unknown

58. "We all eat, and it would be a sad waste of opportunity to eat badly." - Anna Thomas

59. "A restaurant is a place where you can sit down and relax, and let someone else do the cooking for you." - Unknown

60. "Eating is not just a material pleasure. Eating well gives a spectacular joy to life." - Elsa Schiaparelli

61. "Food is like a language, it communicates so much." - Unknown

62. "People who love to eat are always the best people." - Julia Child

63. "The fondest memories are made when gathered around the table." – Unknown

64. "A restaurant is a fantasy—a kind of living fantasy in which diners are the most important members of the cast." - Warner LeRoy

65. "I judge a restaurant by the bread and by the coffee." - Burt Lancaster

66. "The most essential part of my day is a proper dinner." - Rachael Ray

67. "A restaurant should remove you from the mundane burdens of everyday life and transport you to another world." - Danny Meyer

68. "The only thing I like better than talking about food is eating." - John Walters

69. "Food is not just eating energy. It's an experience." - Guy Fieri

70. "A restaurant is a place where you go to celebrate a special occasion, or to create a new one." - Unknown

71. "Food is our common ground, a universal experience." - James Beard

72. "There is no love sincerer than the love of food." - George Bernard Shaw

73. "There is no better feeling in the world than a warm pizza box on your lap." - Kevin James

74. "Good food is good mood." - Unknown

75. "Eating is a necessity but cooking is an art." - Unknown

76. "A bad day can be made better with some good food." - Unknown

77. "Food is the ingredient that binds us together." - Unknown

78. "We all eat, and it would be a sad waste of opportunity to eat badly." - Anna Thomas

79. "A restaurant is a place where you can sit down and relax, and let someone else do the cooking for you." - Unknown

80. "Eating is not just a material pleasure. Eating well gives a spectacular joy to life." - Elsa Schiaparelli

81. "Food is like a language, it communicates so much." - Unknown

82. "People who love to eat are always the best people." - Julia Child

83. "The fondest memories are made when gathered around the table." - Unknown

84. Although a great restaurant experience must include great food, a bad restaurant experience can be achieved through bad service alone. Ideally, service is invisible. You notice it only when something goes wrong. – Dana Spiotta

85. I'm working harder than ever now, and I'm putting on my pants the same as I always have. I just get up every day and try to do a little better than the day before, and that is to run a great restaurant with great food, great wine, and great service. That's my philosophy. –Emeril Lagasse

86. Although the skills aren't hard to learn, finding the happiness and finding the satisfaction and finding fulfilment in continuously serving somebody else something good to eat, is what makes a really good restaurant. – Mario Batali

87. Profit is not the legitimate purpose of business. The legitimate purpose of business is to provide a product or service that people need and do it so well that it's profitable. – James Rouse

88. "When you are able to shift your inner awareness to how you can serve others, and when you make this the central focus of your life, you will then be in a position to know true miracles in your progress toward prosperity." – Wayne W. Dyer

89. The best way to find yourself is to lose yourself in the service of others. – Mahatma Gandhi

90. To give real service you must add something which cannot be bought or measured with money, and that is sincerity and integrity. – Douglas Adams

91. The sole purpose of business is service. The sole purpose of advertising is explaining the service which business renders. – Leo Burnett

92. Earn your success based on service to others, not at the expense of others. – H. Jackson Brown, Jr.

93. Always render more and better service than is expected of you, no matter what your task may be. – Og Mandino

94. Service which is rendered without joy helps neither the servant nor the served. But all other pleasures and possessions pale into nothingness before service which is rendered in a spirit of joy. – Mahatma Gandhi

95. Joy can only be real if people look upon their life as a service and have a definite object in life outside themselves and their personal happiness. – Leo Tolstoy

96. The path to your own happiness is usually found in service. – Jonathan Lockwood Huie

97. Consists in giving, and in serving others. – Henry Drummond

98. A generous heart, kind speech, and a life of service and compassion are the things which renew humanity. – The Buddha

99. "Men are rich only as they give. He who gives great service gets great rewards." – Elbert Hubbard

100. The customer experience is the next competitive battleground. – Jerry Gregoire

Closing Thoughts

As we conclude this culinary journey, "The Restaurant Blueprint: A Guide to Starting, Sustaining, and Scaling Successful Restaurants," stands as a beacon for both aspiring restaurateurs and seasoned industry professionals. The pages within have woven together a tapestry of practical insights, strategic frameworks, and real-world examples, providing a comprehensive guide and invaluable resource.

From conceptualizing a unique culinary vision to mastering the intricacies of operations, marketing, and customer experience, this book has equipped readers with the knowledge and tools necessary to navigate the dynamic landscape of the restaurant business successfully. The principles outlined here, rooted in timeless wisdom, continue to be relevant in an ever-evolving culinary world that embraces innovation, Green Restaurant practices and adapts to changing consumer preferences.

Whether you are embarking on a new culinary venture or seeking to revitalize an existing establishment, the strategies and wisdom shared within these pages will undoubtedly contribute to the success and sustainability of your restaurant endeavour. May this book serve as a guiding light, inspiring culinary entrepreneurs to create memorable dining experiences and play an integral role in the vibrant tapestry of the restaurant industry.